Grow fruit in your greenhouse

Typical grapes and peaches grown in a small greenhouse.

Grow fruit in your greenhouse

Grapes, peaches, nectarines, figs, and others

George E. Whitehead

FABER AND FABER · London

First published in 1970
by Faber and Faber Limited
3 Queen Square London WC1
Reissued 1973
Printed in Great Britain by
Unwin Brothers Limited
The Gresham Press Old Woking Surrey

ISBN 0 571 09298 5

So curious and cunning are our gardeners now in these days that they presume to do in manner what they list with Nature, and moderate her course in things as if they were her superiors.

WILLIAM HARRISON (1593)

Acknowledgements

It is impossible to compile a work of this sort without the help and goodwill of others. Among those who have been of personal assistance are; Alison Ross, who drew most of the sketches; Graham Whitehead, my nephew, who drew the greenhouse plans; Ron Oulds, who took special photographs, including the cover picture; R. F. Strawson of G. F. Strawson and Son, for allowing me to use two photographs from their catalogue; and Pamela Harrington, who typed the original and re-typed the amended script.

I also appreciate the help given by the staff of the R.H.S. Gardens, Wisley, and in particular their advice concerning the use of pesticides.

There are others I cannot personally acknowledge. They are the anonymous people who do everything to convert the raw material of the manuscript into a publishable book. Without them we who are privileged to write would seldom get very far. To all I am grateful.

GEORGE E. WHITEHEAD

Contents

Illustrations

Plates

Figures

Introduction

This book has two main objectives. One is to help those who aspire to grow choice fruit in small greenhouses the proper way, i.e. if starting from scratch, by studying the right type of house, the most modern equipment and the most suitable vines or trees.

The second idea is rather more ambitious. It is to suggest to the thousands of owners of small greenhouses who have failed to make the best use of them that they are more likely to succeed with fruit than with any other sort of plant.

We must remember that grapes, peaches, nectarines and figs are almost hardy in this country. In fact, ever since they were introduced a constant flow of writers, mainly amateurs, have explained how to grow them outdoors.

However, strive as they will, they must admit, if they are honest, that it is a struggle outdoors, whereas, if these fruits are given glass protection they are superior in quality and more reliable in cropping.

There is a misconception that grapes, and peaches, need considerable heat. The old establishments in which I started my gardening career mostly had ranges of fruit houses fitted with elaborate heating systems. They created this misconception. But now with modern appliances hardly any heat is needed at all, provided that crops are not wanted very much out of season.

It is possible to dispense with heat throughout winter, and it will be found that grapes and peaches benefit by frosts. Figs like a winter climate too, but are best kept free from freezing, although disease is often the cause outdoors, when cold is blamed.

The main reason why owners of small, cheap greenhouses find that they are unable to fulfil their aspirations is the fluctuation in temperatures that occurs in houses inadequately ventilated or controlled. The plants cannot stand it. There are other minor problems such as the constant watering. While modern auto-

15

matic aids are helping to overcome such drawbacks, they do not ordinarily remove unending vigilance.

But, if some of the best modern automatic aids are applied, especially if adjustments to the house structure are made to growing these fruits, there need be less constant attention than for other subjects. I cannot think of anything else that can be left unattended throughout winter.

Growing indoor fruit the cool way is not a new idea, although it has not been universally practised. But I have proved it very rewarding. When the Second World War started we had to jettison two heated vineries in order to grow other edible crops without any artificial heat. But I had compassion on a 'Foster's Seedling' vine, it being behind the water tank, and giving little trouble. After the second cold winter it gave better crops than ever it did when the masses of pipes were kept heated. It has its roots completely inside the house and is still bearing well.

When I was much younger I was fortunate to have some wonderful friends who took immense pride in the cultivation of indoor fruit and plants. One of these was Fred Rose, who was a very successful national exhibitor of grapes and peaches, and who contributed the notes upon the cultivation of indoor vines in the Royal Horticultural Society's *Dictionary of Gardening*. He gave clearly in those notes his views on keeping vines cold during winter.

Another wonderful friend was Francis Hanger, at that time in charge of the famous Exbury Gardens. I was in charge of Cadland, situated between Exbury and Townhill Park, where Fred Rose grew his fruit. It was in their company I gained much knowledge.

Still another great friend who helped me very considerably was J. Wilson, who was always keenly interested in the cultivation of indoor fruit. After becoming an advisory consultant on the Royal Horticultural Society's staff, he wrote the *Guide to the Cultivation of Apricots, Peaches, Nectarines, Figs and Grapes*.

In this book, not only have I tried to explain in realistically simple terms how indoor fruits are generally cultivated, both in the preparation and the maintenance of the vines and plants, but I have also strived to impart that power of understanding plants that a successful gardener manages to attain. It is not easy to write in this way. So often those who want to grow fruit and other plants demand definite rules, such as set temperatures to be kept, amount of food to give, and a rigid timetable. Far better is it to gain a general idea of what various plants like, and then to use one's discretion. Again, in the *Dictionary of Gardening*, Fred Rose strove to impart that feeling that one acquires by realising that those things that live in greenhouses are living individuals. When he walked into his vineries he looked at the vines rather than the thermometer.

Vines have been given the major share of room in this book, not because they are difficult, but because the cultivation of them is a fascinating pastime. Also, much of the information about the preparation of the houses and the borders for them is equally applicable to peaches, nectarines, and figs. The book is intended to be read as a whole rather than sectionalised according to the subject.

PART ONE
Grapes

1—Grapes: Brief History and Varieties

Although the ancient Egyptians recorded that wine was made from grapes 6,000 years ago, and there is endless literature upon the subject, as well as records of outdoor vineyards (including one near where I am writing this), it was not until 250 years ago that heated vineries became a reality. This revolution began, as did many gardening discoveries, in large estate gardens, at that time much more widespread than now.

During this comparatively short period, the development of the indoor grape attained extraordinary popularity, reaching its zenith about a century ago.

At first, the discovery that vines under glass would grow to exceptional size created a friendly rivalry among the gardeners of the period, some experts becoming famous and one at least still having his name revered by a fertiliser.

In those days it was usual for the vinery to be built to the needs of the vines rather than fitting the vines to the existing structure which we now normally do.

But the vines did not flourish everywhere. The gardener, be as expert as he was, could make them grow in one garden with miraculous vigour, but in another fail to obtain other than a poor response.

It was soil, and drainage, that had much to do with it. All those vines had natural root runs, and most of them flourished where it was of an alluvial nature, especially if the soil was gravelly and calcareous as well.

Hampton Court Vine

One of the favoured localities was along the Thames Valley near London. Here is still the famous Hampton Court Vine. Other nearly famous vines included those at Cumberland Lodge, Windsor Park, Sillwood, Sunninghill, and at Valentines, Ilford, Essex. The Edinburgh district of Scotland was also the home of several large vineries.

'Black Hamburgh' was the variety most favoured, because it responded so nobly to the open root-run system. A fine example is the specimen at Hampton Court. A vine at Valentines was planted in 1758 and became the parent plant of the more renowned Hampton Court offshoot that was planted in 1769. This still flourishes exceedingly, and has now attained its second century of yielding a yearly heavy crop, on which newspapers report every late summer.

At the time of writing this it is being carefully tended by a dedicated lady gardener, for this massive specimen, except for the main stump, which has a girth of several feet, is looking as fresh and healthy as a youngster.

Of course, the glass structure is perfect, and has obviously been renewed from time to time. Although this has been kept more or less within the original area, the roots have been carefully nurtured outside the house.

We are told that they run farther and wider than the very extensive clear beds specially reserved for them. But, undoubtedly, it is the feeding and mulching that has kept this vine in such a vigorous health. The floor of the interior is comparatively dry and sandy, and suggests that all the roots are outside—but how far is difficult to assess accurately. I wish the reader to note this because it will be commented upon later when we deal with problems such as 'shanking' and 'adventitious rooting'.

The Manresa Vine

The most impressive vine that I know about was at Manresa House, Roehampton, where it was started from an 'eye' in 1862, and grown on in a three-quarter-span greenhouse that had to be specially made for it, the length being 224 ft. It was trained to form seven horizontal 'rods' the full length of the house, thus making over 500 yd. of rod-length in all. It produced 2,500 bunches annually, but these were reduced to 700, and yielded in the region of a ton of grapes each year. The amazing thing about all this is that it was the same gardener, Mr. M. Davis, who raised the vine from an 'eye' and managed to bring it to this state of perfection.

His treatment for the Manresa vine was different to that given to the Hampton Court vine. It had a free root run, just as does the one at Hampton Court. But it was encouraged to grow in the borders inside the house, rather than outside. Undoubtedly, it also sent its roots in search of additional food farther afield. But the main sustenance consisted of frequent dressings of fresh horse droppings, sprinkled with water from time to time, to give off ammonia, as well as provide goodness for the roots. This, undoubtedly, accounted for the prodigious growth of that vine. A vine grown that way can last for many years, but there comes a time when the bed becomes soured and saturated and causes the roots to deteriorate.

The Heaviest Bunch

While some gardeners strove after the heaviest crop, others preferred to have the largest bunches. Unfortunately, many of the varieties that produced these were of inferior quality, consequently they were often given unjustifiable prominence.

However, the very popular and excellent 'Black Hamburgh' has produced some unusually large bunches. One grown at Durham in 1874 weighed over 20 lb.

For records, the white grapes outweigh the black ones, and the variety 'Trebbiano' has yielded a bunch that weighed over 26 lb. Another prodigious bearer of very large bunches is 'White Nice'. One of the largest of this variety ever known weighed slightly more than the 'Trebbiano' effort when it was freshly cut, and measured 2 ft. 3 in. across the shoulders, and was the same length.

There are interesting and amusing stories about indoor grapes, their owners, growers, and feats accomplished. One that appeals to me concerns the Duke of Portland in 1781, sending a bunch of 'White Syrian' as a present to Lord Rockingham at Wentworth House 20 miles away. It weighed 19½ lb. and was carried, suspended, on a staff between two men; the incident, presumably, inspired by the biblical story.

Restricted Beds

The next phase of indoor viticulture occurred when it was found that vines could be grown in restricted spaces, simply by stopping the roots from wandering from a given area. Not only could the top growths then be trained to the system that the gardener preferred but also the roots could be controlled as well. This brought about a different policy for, instead of the gardener producing a prodigious crop off one vine, he could now plant a number of varieties of vines in one house, and so not only have a choice of colour of skin, and flavour, he could spread over the season to the extent of having grapes on the menu throughout the year. He did this with the aid of heating and also a storage room, in which were rows of special bottles, into which the stems of the bunches were inserted and the berries kept fresh by the water supply. I have been in charge of two gardens where there were such rooms.

Obviously there were many varieties tested for indoor cultivation, and many a gardener introduced new ones that were too often found wanting. Some of the best were given many aliases, either through the gardener wishing to pretend that he had found something better than anyone else, or, more often, he had scrounged 'eyes' from other friendly gardeners, who did not wish it to be divulged that they had been helpful, in case it created chagrin among jealous employers.

'Black Hamburgh' and the 'Sweetwater' Varieties

There is no doubt whatever that the variety we know as 'Black Hamburgh' has been, and is, the most popular of all indoor grapes. While it flourishes as a giant vine in an enormous structure, it will likewise bear crops with its roots confined in pots. It was imported from Hamburgh by a John Warner about 1730. He had a vineyard, at Rotherhithe. But it really needs glass protection and the consequent care to bring out the true qualities of the fruit.

Some names that have been given to 'Black Hamburgh' are 'Frankenthal', 'Garston Black', 'Richmond Villa', as well as variations of the original title like 'Dutch Hamburgh' and 'Mill Hill Hamburgh'. The bunches are large with broad shoulders, while berries are round, of good size and slightly oval. The colour is black, the skin is thin, the flesh is firm and tender, sweet and nicely flavoured. Taken altogether, quite a satisfactory grape if there is only one vine to be grown.

When gardeners placed grapes in categories they referred to 'Black Hamburgh' as the best of the Sweetwaters. All these are characterised by thin skins, earliness in ripening, juiciness and sweetness. Some are black—and some white-skinned. A white one often grown is 'Buckland's Sweetwater', and is most favoured for exhibition qualities. But it is not first-class for table. However, it must be pointed out that it has been eulogised by some writers, which leads me to think that much of the quality of good taste is often in the mind. But it can also be due to the sort of soil in which the roots are growing, influencing the flavour to such an extent that grapes can taste good in one garden and mediocre in another.

Another white sweetwater grape is 'Foster's Seedling', which I have grown in a very restricted inside border for over 20 years, the vine still persisting in producing good bunches of grapes. The bunches and the berries are of modest proportions, but ripen attractively, becoming clear as amber. I regard this as the easiest of all indoor grapes to grow, and it is ideal where there are children, for it is sweet, tender-fleshed and juicy. It will thrive in a very restricted root run.

Very often, 'Royal Muscadine' is recommended for unheated houses. Another name for it is 'Chasselas de Fontainbleau'. But it is a variable grape and unless one knows the parent from which it has been propagated, it is somewhat speculative. And, again, it varies with the soil. In firm soil the bunches are compact, while in loose, sandy compost they are smaller, and blunt-ended. The fruit is yellow turning to amber when ripe, and transparent, and covered with a dense white bloom. The flesh is tender and sweet, and there is a perceptible muscat flavour. It is earlier than 'Black Hamburgh', and, when left to shrivel a bit, the flavour is enhanced.

The muscat named 'Madresfield Court' is a good grape for an unheated vinery if the position is warm and sheltered. The handsome black, oblong berries are borne on long tapering bunches that are compactly shouldered. The flesh is tender and juicy and has a suggestion of the traditional muscat flavour. It is ideal for a small house. Its obvious rival, both in earliness and appearances, is 'Black Hamburgh'. Of the two, Hamburgh is much the easiest to grow, but Madresfield exceeds in quality.

There are many less imposing varieties often recommended for cold houses. They flourish outdoors in suitable positions. Examples are 'Gamay Hatif des Vosges', with small black berries, and 'Perle de czaba', whose berries are white. A very good one is 'Chasselas Vibert', with amber-coloured berries that are beautiful and delicious.

The Muscats
Undoubtedly, the muscat grapes are the aristocrats of the vinery.

We have already mentioned 'Madresfield Court', as being suitable for an unheated house. There is also 'Black Muscat', or 'Muscat Hamburgh', or 'Venn's Black', being one and the same. It has excellent flavour, but sets badly, and will start to shank at the least provocation. It is early, and follows closely on 'Black Hamburgh'. I do not think it can compare favourably with 'Madresfield Court'.

The most wonderful of all indoor grapes I consider to be 'Muscat of Alexandria'. I have grown it in heated houses where it produced bunches up to 18 in. long, of large oval berries that are greenish-yellow until turning to golden amber when ripe. The skin is slightly tough, but the flesh crackles, and is sweetly rich, with a real muscat flavour. If synonyms are a criterion, it has been given many names, among them 'Archerfield', 'Bowood Muscat', 'Charlesworth Tokay', 'Muscat Escholata', and 'Tottenham Park'. But it does need considerable heat in the ripening stages. It is not a matter of room space as much as management. With modern heating and moisture control it should appeal to the gardener who loves a challenge.

Where old viticulturalists congregate to discuss the merits of varieties the 'Canon Hall Muscat' will be mentioned before many words have passed. Although 'Muscat of Alexandria' is my choice it has to be admitted that Canon Hall excels in many respects. The bunches are large and bluntly tapering. The berries are larger than usual and bluntly oval. The skin is primrose colour and thin. The flesh is firm and crackles. There is more juice, while the flavour is definitely vinous and musky. In fact, a perfect bunch of 'Canon Hall Muscat' is unsurpassed by any other grape on this earth, but it seldom is perfect. The berries are often irregular, and it must be grown steadily right from the start, and continued so throughout its growing season.

A grape that the inexperienced grower may well consider is 'Gros Colmar', sometimes named 'Gros Colman'. It has medium sized bunches of black grapes that are about the largest in size that I know. The flesh is somewhat coarse and adheres to the thick skins, and not so sweet as many varieties, but once well ripened the flavour becomes vinous and moresome. It is a very easy grape to grow, and to keep healthy year after year. The colour on the skin does not develop fully until late summer, and some heat is necessary for it to be brought to satisfying maturity.

It is a far coarser grape than 'Black Hamburgh', but it is a very good one to extend the season. Another point in its favour is that it will flourish in a house where flowers are growing, and it is necessary to have controlled warmth for them. When the very handsome bunches are hanging below a canopy of reddish leaves, as is their natural hue, the vinery gives an atmosphere of 'harvest home'. This grape is in good company with the biggest marrow in the festival. But, if you are a connoisseur, and can cultivate the muscats, your appreciation of its edible qualities will become much diminished.

There are other late black grapes, well known to experts, but not so frequently cultivated now as in the past. 'Alicante' was so much a favourite that it has at times been named 'Black Lisbon', 'Black St. Peter's', 'Black Tokay', 'Espagnin Noir' and 'Meredith's'. In a cool house the bunches will hang for weeks during the winter. 'Mrs. Pince' is a late muscat. One of the grapes we had in the storage room was 'Lady Downe's', with richly flavoured, vinous, black largish berries. This sounds much more attractive than 'Gros Colmar', for instance, but the snag is in the growing. Of such as these it is enough for me to state that they exist.

There are many old varieties that I have never seen. There are some newer ones of whose existence I am unaware. But generally, and, to some extent, sorrowfully, the number of varieties has receded considerably.

The vineyard grapes, as distinct from those of the vinery, are far more extensive. It would take years of research to seek them out. It is imperative that only the best possible cultivars for the small greenhouse, converted into a vinery, be studied before making a decision.

I end this chapter with opinionated selections.

FOR THE SMALL UNHEATED GREENHOUSE
(in order of preference)

'Black Hamburgh' (August–September)
'Foster's Seedling' (white, August–September)
'Chasselas Vibert' (white, July–August)
(These three can be planted in a mixed vinery,
or cultivated singly)

FOR A SMALL VINERY WITH AUXILIARY HEATING,
SUCH AS AN ELECTRIC TURBINE HEATER

For early ripening

'Black Hamburgh'
'Madresfield Court' (black, mid-August and September)
'Foster's Seedling' (white)

For late ripening

'Gros Colmar' (black, October–November)
'Alicante' (black, October–November)
'Mrs. Pearson'* (white, October–November)

FOR A CORRECTLY HEATED VINERY

'Muscat of Alexandria' (white, October–November)
'Canon Hall Muscat' (white, October–November)
'Mrs. Pince' (black, long-keeping)
'Mrs. Pearson' (white, long-keeping)

Chief periods when artificial heat is needed are spring and when crop is ripening. At these periods a steady night temperature of 60° F. (16° C.) is desirable.

* N.B. 'Mrs. Pearson' is a muscat with tapering bunches of roundish oval berries of amber colour. Flavour is first rate when well ripened but does need considerable warmth in autumn.

2—The Ideal Vinery

If the right conditions are given, I reiterate that there is almost no sort of small glasshouse that cannot be converted into a successful vinery. And, except for a very few that are ill-fated for anything, certain flowers can be grown along with the vines, and be all the better for the alterations that have to be made. The best way to tackle this subject, I think, is to study the whys and wherefores of a traditional vinery.

Just before the First World War there were many of them to be found in estate gardens, in all sizes, shapes and condition, all over the country. Some were fitted with many unnecessary refinements, but all had certain essential features that we should consider.

By studying the old, and yet including some of the newest aids to cultivation we can go about this undertaking with confidence.

As already ascertained in the first chapter, there were two definite and distinct forms of cultivation. The original way was to plant the vine in the local soil, just as though it were a native climber and let it ramp, but training its shape and increasing the size of the vinery until it attained gigantic proportions, or it perished.

But, for the small grower, it is better to adhere to a later form of cultivation, where the roots are enclosed in beds in keeping with the size of the vinery. This has many advantages. The crop can be spread over a long period, even when the vinery is small, for there can be a number of varieties.

Incidentally, I have worked where we had three smallish vineries that enabled us to have grapes available throughout the year. There was the early house which was well heated to force the crop of early varieties. There was the mid-season, containing the choicest muscats, and a late house, in which were grown those varieties that were slow to mature and would keep well in the grape room.

29

Borders

Now let us consider the enclosed borders in which the roots can spread. There are three types. There is the border with the roots kept within the vinery. There is the vinery with all the roots outside. Then we have the inside-cum-outside border, the main roots being inside, but spreading through arches into enclosed outdoor beds.

The early forcing houses generally had their borders completely inside because it was thought necessary for the roots to be kept just as warm as the interior of the vinery. Late slow-growing varieties were retarded by keeping the roots completely outside,

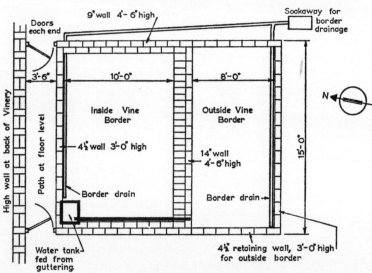

FIG. 1. Ground plan of lean-to vinery

while the interior of the vinery was ventilated as much as possible until growth began. The mid-season, and the choicer varieties, either had their roots entirely indoors or were indoor-cum-outdoor.

In my opinion the best combination is having both indoor and outdoor borders together. As we shall find, it enables the grower to develop the productivity of the vine steadily, but surely, over several years.

30

The advantage of an all-outside border is that the floor of the interior can be used for plants, which it cannot be when full of roots. But before jumping to decisions that sound attractive, the reader is advised to study the needs of the vine, as discussed later, for it may be impracticable to please both the vines and the plants regarding their respective climatical needs. It all depends upon the sort of plants.

However, to develop the theme of the simple, yet efficient vinery, I have outlined the ground plan (Fig. 1) that would suit an ideal lean-to greenhouse 15 ft. long, alongside the solid wall to which it is fixed, and with a projection of 13½ ft. from the wall. To it has been added an outside border 8 ft. across, thus making a complete vinery 15 ft. long and 21½ ft. from back wall to front including the outside bed.

It will be noted that the wall at the back is running from east to west, and that the vinery is on the south side. This is because vines love sunshine. They can never have too much.

Path and Doors

The path is next to the wall. Doors have to be fitted, these generally being of half panelling below and glass lights above. They open inwards.

It is just one of those quirks that old private greenhouses had doors that opened inwards, while the commercial counterparts invariably have them to open outwards. The main reason for this is utilitarian. The private greenhouse is akin to a living-room, whereas a commercial house is like a stable. The latest doors are sliding. I do not like them.

The south side of the vinery path is bounded by the retaining wall of the inside border. It is approximately 3 ft. high. It can be a little higher, rather than lower.

Supporting Walls

The low 3-ft. brick retaining walls do no more than keep the sides of the soil borders intact. But there are also the main supporting walls upon which the wooden frame of the greenhouse is placed. These have to be wider and more substantial.

This is plainly revealed on the plan. In almost all cases they used to be very solid indeed. Bricks were patterned to make a wall 14 in. wide at the base, and then tapered up so that the top layer was only one brick laid lengthwise—4½ in. The reason for this narrowing was that it enabled the builder to place the base of the framework so that it overlapped the outside edge. There was a drip groove made upon the lower side of the overlapping beam, to stop the underflow of rainwater, thus preventing it from seeping into the crevice between bricks and wood. A strip of felt was also laid over the brickwork.

The heavy solid brickwork gave warmth and solidity to the structure. It enabled arches under the front wall to be built without fear of collapse. Just for conformity, 14-in. walls were also used at the ends of the house. In my plan I have given a width of 9 in., which is ample.

With modern concrete blocks this heavy form of construction is unnecessary, but I describe what used to be done, and why.

Generally, the walls that supported the woodwork were only 18 in. higher than the retaining walls, hence the height of these is 4½ ft., from the floor surface below the borders to the single-row brick top upon which the structure is placed.

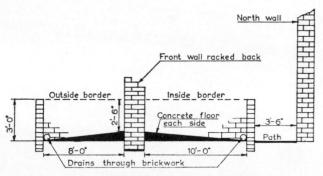

FIG. 2. Showing slope of floor surface

The Floor

The floor itself was of pounded down chalk, or gravel, and was ample on ground that could not be penetrated by vine roots. However, to make sure, it is best made with concrete. It is easier to lay.

The floor can be laid first, if preferred, and the walls built over it. I personally prefer to dig foundations for main walls and build them up part of the way before filling in the floor. Otherwise I am going to be involved in levels that may go wrong.

The floor should be sloped each way from the front wall to the extremities of the beds each side, as in Fig. 2. The best depth of the bed is 2½ ft. alongside the front wall, and 3 ft. at the edges. Thus there is a fall of 6 in. I find it easier to put in that floor after the main walls have been started, but before they are completed. The retaining walls can be laid upon the concrete floor later.

This is purely strategy. I hasten to assure the reader that the whole operation is not over-laborious, nor complicated. It is very practical, and once done, will last for several decades.

When converting an existing greenhouse much of this is inapplicable, as we shall see. But, if one is investing in a proper vinery, this information can be most helpful.

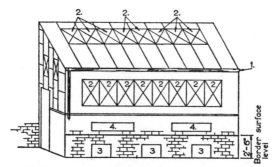

1: Rain gutter with down-pipe led thro' wall to tank inside.
2: Pivoted sashes and roof lights for ventilation.
3: Arches,(outside border, and soil hiding arches not shown.)
4: Wooden hinged or sliding ventilators.

FIG. 3. Showing arches under front of vinery and wooden ventilators in brickwork

Water Tank

An interior tank is most advisable. Vines love soft rain water that is of the same temperature as the vinery. It can be collected by having guttering along the eaves, fitted with stack pipes leading through a hole in the brickwork down inside the tank.

The best position for the tank is beside the path, sitting flatly on the floor, with its rim just low enough to give a sufficient fall to the inflow pipe.

Underground Arches

Before we consider the main structure, we must deal with the front wall brickwork, or concrete walling, therefore Fig. 3 is next for comment. It consists of the lower walling in which are three arches.

A lean-to greenhouse 15 ft. long is ample for three vines grown on the single-rod upright system. The vines are planted inside the vinery, but the roots will eventually be allowed to expand their roots into the outer border by growing through those arches. The arches are 2 ft. deep from floor to top, thus being 6 in. below border surface level.

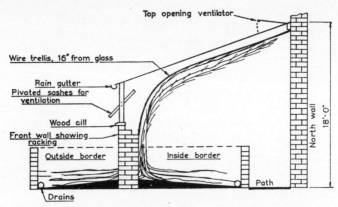

FIG. 4. General elevation of lean-to vinery

The base of the wall structure between the arches is 14 in. wide (if of the old style), but tapers upwards inside, to 4½ in. upon which the wood structure is placed. That can be clearly seen in Fig. 4.

However, it will be noticed that in the top bricks (Fig. 3) are two wooden shuttered ventilators. These are refinements in old vineries, often unnecessary if modern heating and ventilators are adopted. But they may help us when we are converting difficult houses. That is mainly why they are included in the drawing for future reference.

Drainage

It should always be remembered that vines grow best when the roots are on dryish bottoms, although they do need quite a lot of water. Therefore, we must give them plenty at certain seasons and yet it should flow away if we are over-generous.

In Fig. 1 there is a form of outside drainage, which takes surplus water away from the lowest parts of the beds at the south and north extremities. This flows through holes made in the lowest course of bricks at the appropriate points.

But also inside, close to the retaining walls, another row of pipes should be laid to catch the overflow off the sloped bed. In addition to that there is also a layer of rubble or pebbles, quite 4 in. deep, laid over the whole floor, which acts in the same way as crocks in a pot.

As we shall see, if we prepare the beds and plant the vine in the prescribed way, all this need not be done at once, nor need the outside border be made for two or three years if there is also an inside one, but I must not dwell on that further at this stage, or I will confuse.

The outside drain and soakaway mentioned need not be necessary if the borders are above garden level. But there must be the drainage facilities within the borders, with outlets that will enable the surplus water to drain from the vinery floor.

Main Structure

Fig. 4 plainly shows us a cross-section of the whole vinery in which we can see the shape of the front brickwork, with the overlapping wood base, and the pivotal sashes above, reaching to the eaves and rain gutter, as well as the other important features.

But firstly, I draw attention to the slope of the roof. In my opinion the best angle is one of about 30 degrees. If it is steeper it allows heat from the sun to enter more rapidly, but it also causes the vinery to become cold more quickly in the evening. It also makes the business of thinning the bunches and giving other attentions more difficult than if the roof is less steep. If it is at a flatter angle changes of temperature are less erratic, but there is danger of drop from condensation. Also, water may flow back under the panes of glass when it rains heavily. Still another drawback to a flat roof is that bunches are damaged by being brushed when passing under them, and a still further reason for not having a flatter roof is that it restricts the growing space.

Supports

We now look at the normal fittings that support the vines. Actually, the vine rods have to be secured to a wire framework

35

that stretches from just above the ground to the apex of the roof. This consists of strong vertical iron bars bent to the shape of the front and roof, held strongly in position to the main structure, in which are eyeholes through which the horizontal straining wires are threaded and made taut, thus making a reliable trellis.

In the ideal house the wires are held about 16 in. below the glass. This enables a free air flow between bottom and top ventilators, and also reduces the chances of scorching, or damage to the young foliage when it touches the glass.

However, very few greenhouses are large enough for that amount of free space. The trellis is more often about 12 in. from the glass. I have seen it as close as 9 in. But it is not good.

The horizontal wires are spaced about 10–12 in. above each other. I have seen them closer, but they are more difficult to work between. About a foot apart is best for holding upright rods.

The larger vines most often have the main rods (stems) running horizontally along the wires instead of up and across them. The gigantic vines mentioned earlier have them that way. These are spaced about 2 ft. apart. One can either have intersecting wires between those that carry the rods, so spacing them a foot apart, or leave them 2 ft. asunder. I prefer to have the extra wires to support the new growths and bunches.

While for the ideal vinery, undoubtedly, the upright single rod form of growth is best, it is likely that certain small houses will best accommodate grapes if the horizontal system is adopted. This and other forms of training vines are dealt with in Chapter 4.

If you are buying a new vinery or fruit house you will naturally insist that the straining wires are fitted by the manufacturers. There are firms fully conversant regarding this necessary equipment. Most of them are prepared to moderate their designs to suit your special wishes.

I regard the installation of straining wires, to form a suitable trellis, the biggest problem that has to be overcome when converting ordinary greenhouses to the growing of fruit.

It is not necessarily the cheapest houses that are the most impracticable in this respect. Some of the finer metal types are so fragile that it is dangerous to fit them with wires, especially at the correct distance from the glass. When obtaining a new vinery or peachery, this is a very important factor to bear in mind.

For houses with a wooden framework, the usual way is to fix

strong angle irons to the inside of the end walls at the optimum distance from the roof. These should run from near the ground, up to the apex or ridge of the house in a graceful curve, rather than bend sharply at the eaves. They have eyeholes drilled through them at the spaces the wires are to go so that these can be threaded through and secured tautly. There are also steel pins screwed into the main rafters where needed, with eyes at the ends through which the wires are threaded.

Some metal houses can be drilled through at the ends, but, if fittings cannot be supplied by the manufacturers, the best recourse is a local blacksmith who can generally do what is necessary.

Ventilators

We now look at ventilators. The old vineries were marvellous in this respect, whereas the modern small greenhouses are often appalling.

Plants cannot grow well when temperatures fluctuate, therefore the only means of control is by making openings in the building so that air and heat can intermix with the outer world. This applies to every type of greenhouse for every form of plant life.

It is the main cause for so many optimistic purchases becoming frustrating failures. Still, it can be overcome in most instances, and certainly if fruit is grown instead of flowers.

However, let us pursue the perfect ventilators for our ideal vinery. In Fig. 4, under the eaves, a pivotal sash can be seen which, when operated by an indoor lever from the pathway, opens so that its top goes inwards and its lower half outwards. This, when fully opened, allows a stream of air to enter to flow up between the wire trellis and glass to the escape ventilator at the ridge top. Both ventilators extend right along the front and ridge ensuring little or no draught. It is good.

In some vineries there are variations of the fittings. There can be, for example, hinged ventilators under the eaves instead of the pivotal type. Then, instead of having hinged ventilators at the ridge, there are sliding sashes that open and shut just like those of house bay windows. These are fitted with sashcords and weights that dangle down the back wall, being lifted up and down as to a degree to suit the temperature of the vinery according to the outside weather.

However, there are times when the outer air is so chilling that to open either front sashes or ridge ventilators together would be dangerous to young growths in spring. To overcome that, the old vineries invariably were fitted with apertures in the brickwork under the front sashes, as in Fig. 3, especially those with no outside borders.

The person who first thought of that was a genius. He built them low down, so that they were just above border surface level, but below the hot-water pipes, so that, when opened, either by sliding lids or hinged shutters, the inflowing air was tempered by the pipes before it spread into the house.

They are still most useful in modern ideal vineries, although not quite so essential, as we now have other heating systems, but the idea is a godsend for those who want to overcome the miserable arrangements in some mass-produced houses, as we shall see when we review them in the Supplementary Notes at the end of the book.

Heating

Probably one of the most awe-inspiring features of old-time greenhouses, and especially vineries, were the masses of hot-water pipes encumbering the interiors, taking up much space, and needing constant unstinted attention to furnaces in dungeon-like 'glory-holes'.

They did the job. But they were very wasteful and costly. And they were not always as practical as one would expect. One could not work up a heat to reach the extremity of the pipe-run fast enough on a cold night. The only way was to keep the fire going at full heat all the time, using the ventilators to let out excessive warmth.

Although many manufacturers produce comparative statistics showing that various heating arrangements with several available fuels, and different forms of transference, are superior to electricity and proving it to be the most expensive form of heating, I prefer it to any other in a house that contains vines or peaches of the most popular varieties ripening in a normal season.

Modern oil-burning systems, whether they are with heated water pipes, or are polythene air ducts, or combinations of electricity and oil consumption, are best for commercial growers with large houses, but they are generally too large and costly for houses that are only 20 ft. long, or less. Such systems require careful installation, needing the manufacturer's guidance to install them.

Vines, and to a lesser degree peaches, are improved when they are given the coldest treatment possible during the shortest months of the year. The ventilators should be opened widely from the time the leaves drop in late autumn until the buds begin to swell again in spring. Therefore, there is a vast saving of heating costs just when they are the heaviest for other plants.

There is little artificial heat needed during a normal summer. The only times it is advantageous are spring and autumn, or when there is a cold snap, in an abnormal season. I am positive that there is nothing more useful, easy to manage, and inexpensive to obtain, than an electric fan heater with a built-in thermostat. There are several types, the one I prefer having continuous fan, day and night, but which switches off the heat only at the temperature at which you set it to do so.

The drawbacks are that the current may fail, or a too dry atmosphere is created, or running expenses are too high. These are unlikely to be more than for any other form of heating. And most certainly, there is nothing safer. However, all electrical plug points in greenhouses *must* be fitted specially by a qualified electrician, this expense probably being the heaviest of all. That will be far, far less costly than the installation of most other heating apparatus.

The fan heater is a perfect answer to the temporary heating of any small inexpensive house, for whatever purpose used. You switch on. It keeps the air circulating when not heating it, and checks many of the surface troubles that afflict vines and peaches and other plants.

Other Plants

I said earlier that the ideal vinery 16 ft. long would accommodate three vines spreading from the border towards the top of the roof. This leaves a bare wall at the back. It is often suggested that vines be grown on this wall as well. But that is impracticable, for the bunches need hanging space, and training the growths is difficult. Rather would I erect shelving on the wall face for other plants. Provided we have plants that do not need warmth during December, January and February, many sorts can be grown.

I have raised bedding plants, transplanting them into boxes and keeping them in the vinery. I have also housed on the pathway, or on the free parts of the beds, late-flowering chrysanthemums. Tuberous begonias can also be grown on those shelves.

I have a friend who has a peach tree, a vine and a fig in the same house along with fuchsias. But the vine suffers because it does not get a cold enough winter.

Peach trees will grow on the back walls of a vinery if there is enough room for the roots. In fact it is a good arrangement for a house with a three-quarter span roof, as Fig. 6 shows.

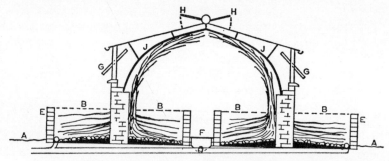

FIG. 5. Cross-section of a span-roof vinery with
inside-cum-outside borders

A–Ground level
B–Level of borders
C–Drainage in borders
D–Outside drainage
E–Border retaining walls

F–Pathway between inner retaining
   walls with grid over drain
G–Side light ventilators
H–Top light ventilators
J–Supporting trellis for vine

(Roof ridge should run north to south)

Some gardeners contend that such a shape is better than a true lean-to for vines, but I prefer just a plain slanting roof if the back wall is high enough to take it. It takes up the least amount of electricity, or whatever fuel is used, than when part of the roof is exposed to the north.

But when all is considered, the only true vinery is one exclusively devoted to grapes, and then it should be of the span-roofed type, as Fig. 5 shows. If for early crops or for the special muscats, or for any crop really, it has to be fitted with the conventional heating apparatus, as well as all the other features so far mentioned.

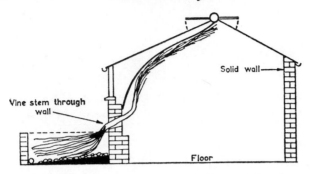

FIG. 6. Section of three-quarter span (or 'hip-roofed') vinery with outside border only, so that interior can be used for other subjects. Path and door can be close to back wall or down centre. Should face due south

Generally the inside borders are drained to a deepish duct underneath the iron-grid middle path, which means that there must be a proper outside drainage system as well. And there must be adequate tankage to store the rain water for use when it is most needed—the dry periods. In one such range of vineries, we had a large underground tank, from which we pumped the water into the smaller tanks inside the houses as needed.

Such edifices are all very well where the costs are of secondary importance. They are, so to speak, an epitome of indoor viticulture. Yet, when these were being evolved, many gardeners were growing the same varieties of grapes quite well in makeshift frames and cloches, so accommodating is the vine that it will thrive in extremes of luxury or pent-up poverty. Yet the grower has to give them the right sort of treatment in each instance, if they are to be kept productive for many years.

3—Preparing and Planting the Vinery

Having dealt with the structure satisfactorily, we now consider the filling of the border with soil for the roots to grow in, and then how to introduce the plants.

It is best not to fill the spaces all at once, but to do so by degrees, spreading the operation over a number of years according to the size of the border, or whether it is inside, outside, or inside-cum-outside.

There are several reasons for this spread-over; much the same as for potting plants. First, you put plants into small receptacles and then gradually into larger ones. If you do not the unused soil becomes sour and unacceptable by the time the roots need it. And also, by confining the roots in a concentrated space they seem to thrive better, will live longer and have better crops.

Most textbooks tell you how to lift the roots of ailing vines, and put notches in them to cause rootlets to form after renewing the soil. This is very much a gimmick that can be completely averted by making new borders in annual stages, rather than giving them the full root run in the first place.

When the border is of the inside-cum-outside type the first thing is to barricade the designed arches so that the soil cannot spill through until we need to develop the outer bed. The barricades of wood, or anything else, such as asbestos sheeting, should be upon the outside so that they can be removed easily in due course.

The first section inside the house should be 3 ft. from front wall towards the path as in Fig. 7, thus giving a border that is a yard across and 2½ ft. deep, for the first year's root run.

In the second year, if the vines have grown well, they are given an additional 2-ft. filling of the inside border. If they have not done so well, only a 1-ft. width is added. And this is repeated, year by year, until all the space of the inside border is filled to the pathway. Then a year later the barricades are removed from the

42

arches, and the outer border is filled in precisely the same way—either by 2-ft. or 1-ft. widths, as deemed necessary for the vines.

Of course, if the border is entirely outdoors, the first strip is made 3 ft. wide, for this is necessary for the initial year. We must remember that the soil is more shallow immediately below the main stems or rods and the roots will spread considerably.

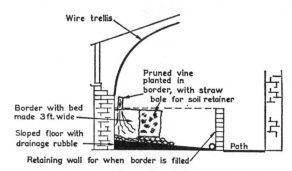

FIG. 7. Section of border planted with vine—first season

The strips of borders are most often held up upon the exposed side by placing inverted lawn turves to form a wall, after the manner of bricks. But, since bought turves have often been treated with selective weedkillers, and there may be residues of these in new turves, I am always chary of using them.

Instead, one of the best retainers is a row of common straw trusses (preferably not treated with weedkiller) placed end to end as in Fig. 7. When placed on the rubble laid over the floor to give bottom drainage they are just the right depth. They are soft yet firm, and any water spilled over them will gradually disperse into them in just the right way to create a growing atmosphere.

These trusses may be bound by wire, or with a plastic tie, and are supplied by corn chandlers, or important pet shops. Sometimes a farmer or a local hack stable can supply a few trusses at a reasonable price.

You are always advised to place some litter over the rubble to stop the soil percolating down into it. I recommend that an extra bale of straw be obtained and broken down for this. In subsequent years, one of the old bales will be just right for this purpose, while the rest can be composted into manure quite well.

Soil Mixture

By extending the making of the entire border over several years the labour and expense of getting soil is eased considerably. Nevertheless, the making of the first section does involve some initial effort. If the vinery is of that ideal size already considered, i.e. 16 ft. long, it will mean obtaining about 10 cu. yd. of soil, or compost, about 2 yd. of drainage rubble and about five bales of straw, or 100 turves.

It is difficult to be dogmatic about the quality or type of soil. You can easily buy expensive stuff that is worse than the soil of your own kitchen garden. Yet the chances are that the soil you have will be unsuitable for this purpose.

Gardeners make a fetish of 'loam'. But there are so many different sorts of loam. By definition it is a mixture of clay, sand and humus, the latter being mostly dead fibrous roots, such as are found in deep-growing grasslands.

When there is a domination of clay it is heavy loam. If this is full of fibre it is 'fat' loam. If it is sandy, and yet contains plenty of fibre, it is light loam. If it contains plenty of chalk it is calcareous loam. Of them all I think that medium loam of a calcareous nature is the best for vines. But it must be fibrous. If it does not contain root fibres, it is marl, which is not ideal for vineries.

Much loam is sterilised by firms who supply John Innes potting mixtures. These are sold by general horticultural sundriesmen. Some are of poor quality. But when considered good, it is worth while finding out whether the same quality loam can be obtained from the same sources. It should not be sterilised.

The drawback with sterilised loam is that it will produce strong, lush vine growths rather than tough, lean and healthy shoots. This is followed by a let-down. But unsterilised loam of a firm yet free texture is just right.

Those of scientific bent will ponder over the alkalinity/acid content as shown by a pH test. While it is better to have an alkaline reaction of above pH 7 than one below, we growers are more concerned about texture. The worst sort of soils are heavy clay, solid chalk and boggy peat. The pH of these can vary to extremes.

The old gardeners who started the growing of wonderful indoor grapes had their own compost recipes, varying in details, but always insisting that the right sort of loam should be the chief ingredient.

The doyen of them all was a Mr. Thompson, whose name is still given to a fertiliser, and who wrote books about the grape a century ago. His formula was:

> 10 barrowloads of medium texture loam
> 1 barrowload of horse droppings
> 2 barrowloads of old mortar
> 1 barrowload of wood-ashes
> 28 lb. of hoof and horn shavings
> ½ cwt. of crushed bones

Another champion grower used:

> 12 barrowloads of medium loam
> 1 barrowload of fresh horse droppings
> 2 barrowloads of old mortar
> 1 barrowload of charcoal nuts
> ½ cwt. of crushed bones

The late Fred Rose, who wrote the notes on the indoor cultivation of the vine in the Royal Horticultural Society's *Dictionary of Gardening*, and who, incidentally, was a delightful friend for many years, gave as his formula 4 parts of loam, 1 part well-rotted manure (parts by volume) and a good sprinkling of wood-ash and bonemeal. He was a very successful exhibition grower.

You note that he did not state the quality of the loam. But that upon the estate where he had his famous gardens was alluvial, and was far better than that normally obtained from any other source.

There are other formulas given in various books. Some advise you to lay turves over the drainage rubble, grass downwards. Some advise you to chop up the mixture into small pieces. Actually, in the old garden, where the loam consisted of local turves cut rather thickly, and stacked in tiers, grass downwards and left for at least a year, it was chopped down with a spade and the ingredients then well mixed in. It was never sifted.

It was always handled when in a moist but not wet condition, for to move it when too dry or wet could spoil the texture.

The old gardeners thought much of fresh horse droppings.

Undoubtedly, it is a good manure for mixing in new borders. I would still use it if obtainable. But when used, care should be taken not to overdo other ingredients, for the loam should always be dominant.

If, after all that, any of these formulas are difficult to follow, there is still the recourse to ready-made proprietary compounds. For example, Bentley's Vine Border Compound, Coarse Grade, if used at the rate of 1 cwt. for each 2 tons of soil, together with 1½ bushels of stick charcoal, are all the additives necessary.

Whatever formula is thought best, or is easiest to obtain, on no account is it wise to make the soil content any richer. To do that courts disappointment and can be disastrous.

You may feel inclined to use your own garden soil. It may work. It may not. As stated earlier, it could possibly be more suitable than that special stuff you buy. It can be porous enough for excess water to drain through easily, and yet be retentive enough to hold the organic and mineral fertilisers that have to be given as the seasons come and go.

The best time to obtain the soil and complete the border is autumn and early winter. This will give a natural settling down period before planting the vines.

Obtaining the Vines

There are many good nurserymen supplying the variety 'Black Hamburgh', but there are not so many who offer interesting collections (see Appendix).

Vines available are mostly in pots, or they are tipped out and put in transit containers with roots still in the original ball of soil. They are generally offered in various ages, the oldest being about five years old. This is a disadvantage.

In my opinion, the best are two-year-olds raised from 'eyes', rather than cuttings. Such plants are rather small but, when planted properly, will surpass the older and larger ones within a few years.

If the order is given in summer they will probably arrive in October. Sometimes they will be pruned back to 6 in. of the base. Sometimes they will not have been pruned, in which case, if they arrive not later than the middle of January, they should be shortened to 6 in., the stem being somewhat thicker than a pencil.

Give as much air as possible, but if the vinery is wanted for other plants, by all means use it, keeping out frost by artificial warmth if necessary.

In early March they can be tipped out of the containers and planted in the border, placing each one in the right position, which should be in the middle of the new border, i.e. 18 in. from the wall, and spaced 5 ft. from its neighbour, or neighbours as the case may be. Dig a deepish hole, and spread out the roots comfortably, covering with soft sedge peat and the border soil. Firm gently, and then soak with tepid water to settle them down.

Keep the house closed, and damp down when the sun shines, and before long the new vines will produce new shoots. Or if they have been planted in an outdoor bed, it is better not to do more than merely plant and water in, in precisely the same way. Should there be a frost once the growths are visible, a temporary covering at night can help them.

Those planted outdoors are placed as near as possible to the vinery wall, rather than in the middle of the bed. If at this stage it is impossible to train them through the hole in the wall that has been made for them, the best new shoot of each plant will have to be trained through directly it can be done comfortably.

The hole in the wall through which the shoot has to be trained should be as close to, but just above, the surface of the border (see Fig. 6).

If young plants arrive in spring, which have not been pruned but are still long and straggly, it is best to plant them without shortening the stems. If they are shortened as late as this they may emit sap through the end, i.e. 'bleed'. However, when they start to grow, the new buds should be removed by rubbing them all off, down to within a foot or so of the base, leaving only those on the lowest part to grow. When the ones left have developed considerable growths and foliage, you can then remove the denuded growth just above the highest shoot that has been allowed to grow. There is none or little bleeding when growth is active and shoots are being formed.

Propagation

It may be that a friend has a specially good vine and you would like to propagate from that. Or you wish to increase your own stock. The usual way to do it is to make a new plant from an 'eye'.

An eye is really a fully developed and mature bud taken from the stem of a one-year-old shoot. It should be healthy and firm. The stem is cut through above and below the eye so that it is about an inch in length. This is placed flat in a small pot of fine soil, in which has been mixed some sedge peat, so that the top of the bud is just discernible through the soil surface. February is the best time for doing this. The bud is kept moist and warm, a temperature of about 70° F. being best.

It will soon form roots, and in due course, say a few weeks, can be repotted into a slightly larger receptacle and be kept growing in the ordinary vinery or greenhouse. In the autumn the top is nipped out because that is the part prone to mildew or die-back in winter. It is repotted into a slightly larger pot during the next spring, and kept growing throughout summer. By the end of summer it will have attained several feet. It is allowed to rest once more, again shortening the unripened shoots, and also, while it is growing in the summer, if any side-shoots form, they are pinched back so that only two or three leaves are left on each one. There should now be one long stem, referred to as a cane.

This can now be planted in the new border as described, taking care first to shorten it to 6 in. in the late autumn when the foliage has fallen. Or it can, if wished, continue to grow in a pot for another year, or two years. It is advisable not to.

The vines grown in the open fields are generally propagated by cuttings inserted directly where they are to grow, much as are black currants, etc. They are trimmed in precisely the same way, with buds left at the extremities of each end, the basal ones being buried in the soil a few inches deep. They form roots easily.

I have also seen indoor vines propagated by cuttings, especially in commercial nurseries. But this form of propagation is deprecated by top-class private growers, who are intent upon obtaining the best quality and biggest crops.

1. A single rod specimen of grape 'Black Hamburgh' when the bunches are just beginning to form. Note the horizontal wires with vertical string attached to form a trellis.

2. An old vine rod showing the bunches of fruit just beginning to form, and also how the shoots are 'stopped' at the tips. Some embryo bunches will be removed later.

4—Training the Vines

The art of training vines is not hard to understand, but it is much easier to do than to describe.

I have already emphasised that the vine is an amazing plant, being amicable to discipline to the extent that it will flourish, if cultivated, to an enormous size, or be confined to a pot. It is this very power of adaptation that can so easily cause things to go wrong.

That they do go wrong in so many instances is evident by the number of vines planted every season, and yet there are so few flourishing vineries. It is primarily due to misconceived ideas, and a failure to understand the reasons for what has to be done instead of relying upon half-learned rule-of-thumb methods.

I must describe the two main methods, yet I earnestly wish to inculcate a power of understanding more than the actual details of operations. These last are comparatively easy, for the vines will grow under many systems if you understand the underlying principles of good growth.

In large vineries, where the roots can run freely, such as that at Hampton Court, the system is to train the very long branches, which are called 'rods', on horizontal wires throughout the length of the structure. But most of us grow them in gardens on one upright rod, similar to a cordon apple tree. This rod has spurs growing from it at the sides, from the lowest wire at the base of the plant, to the extreme tip at the apex.

These spurs produce growths that yield the bunches of grapes amid the leaves far in excess of what they should for our benefit rather than that of the vines. We should remember that Nature imbues practically all vegetation with excessive powers of fecundity, and that we only get good crops when these powers are restricted to the extent that the seed, in this case the stones in the grapes, is wrapped round with the protective flesh that we eat.

No matter what fruit we grow, and especially that where the

D 49

seed is enclosed, the fewer the seeds we allow to form, within reason, the bigger and better is the quality of the flesh.

But this also depends upon other factors. Unless there is vigour in the tree, or in the vine, that fruit cannot swell and become mature. There must be the healthy growth of the shoots, which can only come from good strong buds, or 'eyes', at the ends of the spurs.

Therefore, the grower of grapes, especially indoors, strives to keep a balance by allowing just as much foliage-bearing growth to form to manufacture food for the crop, and to give just enough shade to protect it from excessive heat, or sunshine and, at the same time, to have light.

Some of the shoots growing from the spurs are allowed to produce bunches. Others are not. Those that are allowed to produce them are kept to a proper length by pinching out the growing tip after a few leaves have formed beyond the embryo bunch.

Those that are not allowed to produce bunches have the embryos picked off in the tiny stage. They are also kept to the right length by having the growing tip of each pinched out when it is deemed advisable, and a few leaves have developed.

Furthermore, all the main shoots will produce subsidiary side-shoots, which are described by growers as 'sub-laterals'. These also have their tips pinched out when they have produced three, perhaps four, or five, leaves, according to the general spread and density of the growths as a whole.

Vines vary in their capacity for foliage production. This makes it impossible to be dogmatic. But the idea the grower works for is to have that nice coverage of growths and foliage spread over the wires so that the grapes dangling below can get plenty of light, and yet not be too exposed.

The roots, whether restricted or not, the growth of the rods, the foliage spread, and the crop of grapes must be in balanced harmony. The whole is controlled by judicious treatment. The roots are restricted, and fed, as necessary. The growths are cut back hard to the rods each winter. The new growths (called laterals) are kept short by pinching the growth tips. The bunches are reduced to a reasonable number and grapes in the bunches that are left are thinned.

The other operation, in the early stages, is rubbing off small shoots where branches, growths or laterals, call them what you will, are not wanted.

So far, I have only been generalising with regard to established vines. It stands to reason that vines must develop to that state. In the last chapter, we shortened the planting canes down to within 6 in. of the ground. In the next few paragraphs, we will try to develop from that point.

First Summer

After we planted and pruned the young vine we left the piece we will refer to as the stump. Directly there is enough spring warmth it will start to form shoots around the stem.

If we adopt the single-rod system we only need one of these new shoots to form the rod. Some gardeners, therefore, select the strongest shoot, allowing it to grow, and then rub off the others while tiny with their thumbs. The idea is that all energy goes into this new stem.

However, other gardeners allow all the shoots to grow, willy-nilly, and merely tie them loosely, to some temporary supports until it becomes necessary to sort them out in the winter following the first summer. They argue that growths stimulate roots, and you must have good roots before you can have good tops.

To some extent I agree with that. But if there are several growths, I like to restrict them to from three to five of the best, removing the others by gently rubbing them off where they start from the stump.

Sometimes these three shoots will, during that first season, try to form embryo bunches. These are promptly pinched off. They will also send out side-shoots. These are shortened by pinching out the tips after two leaves have formed. The outcome is that at the end of the first summer, the vine should have three to five long shoots without any subsidiary appendages.

The Second Winter

The tops of these shoots will be somewhat tenuous and soft, and could possibly be mildewed. Whatever they are, the best one of the three is shortened by about half its length (see Fig. 8). The other unwanted four or less are pruned close back to the original stump. Thus, what we have now is the lower part of the new permanent rod.

Should the vine roots be outdoors, and there is insufficient length of stump for the shoot to be pushed through the hole in the wall, it is treated the same way as though indoors, i.e. the usual growths are allowed, these being temporarily tied to stakes, or canes. Then in winter, the best one is pushed through the hole, and shortened by half its length, while the unwanted ones are pruned hard back.

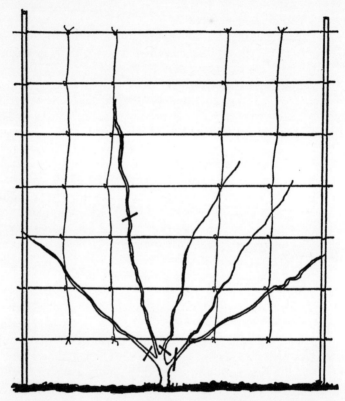

Fig. 8. The first year's growths after planting when restricted to five shoots from the stump. Cuts are made at the points indicated at the end of the season, leaving only half of a stem or cane

Incidentally, the second portion of the border is then filled with the soil. If inside, and there is good strong vine growth, an additional width of 2 ft. is added to the border. If growth is moderate, a foot wide addition is ample. Similarly, if roots are all outdoors, then either a foot, or a 2-ft. width of soil is added to the outdoor border.

Second Summer

When the vines are given the normal spring and summer maintenance, they will start to sprout new side growths from the shortened cane that is now fixed to the underside of the wire trellis under the roof. There should also grow a good new strong shoot at the extremity eventually reaching to the top of the vinery. There may also be many more growing from the stump as well as the rod above it, at all angles.

When they do start, all those below the bottom horizontal wire of the trellis, which means all that are on the original stump, and perhaps one or two at the base of the part that is now the rod, can be rubbed off.

Above that line most of the side-shoots that grow outwards along the wires should be retained so that they are spaced up each side of the rod, in alternating style. They will not necessarily be in alignment with the wires, nor on every wire. But, rather are they alternating upwards as convenient. Any unwanted ones are rubbed off. However, to start with, I cautiously leave more than are essential, pinching out the tips of crowded ones when three leaves have formed.

Should the topmost shoot at the extremity of the pruned rod, that will extend the height, be weaker than the next one below, then it is replaced by the stronger shoot, which is encouraged to take its place.

If the vine is growing well, and the shoots on this lower part of the rod are healthy and strong, one or two bunches of grapes can be allowed to develop. But be very careful not to overload the vine in the beginning. A little reticence in the first years will be rewarded a hundredfold later. We must remember that crops on the lower part of the half-formed rod will rob the top that has still to develop.

All growths from the small spurs on the side of the rod will grow towards the glass, where there is light. They must be gradually pulled back to the wires and fixed by looping over some raffia. This can be tightened gently from time to time as the shoot becomes tougher. But if this is done roughly the break will come at the joint with the spur and there is an irretrievable loss (see Plate 7 of vine with new growths and embryos, bunches of fruit).

Whether bunches are allowed to form or not, the growths are

stopped by pinching out the tips when about 2½ ft. long. They, in turn, will send out side-shoots from the axils, and these are stopped when the third or fourth leaf is formed.

Third Winter

At this stage, before we prune we should have the main cane swelling nicely to form a rod, with growths to right and left, some of which may have borne grapes. Above will be the top half that has only formed during the summer, which may, or may not, have shortened side-shoots.

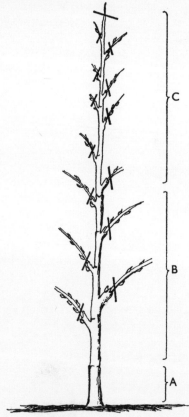

FIG. 9. Where to prune—third winter, i.e. second winter after planting

Key: A, main root or stump; B, first summer's growth after planting;
C, second summer's growth

When all the foliage has fallen in winter the new piece is shortened at the top to the point where the extreme height of the permanent rod is to be just under the apex of the house. Any side-shoots on that top half are also pruned back, close to the stem, only leaving one or two eyes from which next year's growths can come. These points will be the spurs in future years.

The thicker, one-year-old lower half of the rod will already have formed small spurs at the base of the branches that have been trained along the wires and stopped at their appropriate lengths. These are now pruned back to those short spurs, leaving one or two visible buds from which they can start again in the spring (Fig. 9).

Here I want to explain that I always fear breaking off new growths in early summer at the point where they start to grow from the spurs. They sometimes snap off when one is trying to pull them back to the wires. To minimise this I like to allow two growths on each spur if it is possible. The one farthest from the rod is allowed to grow its full $2\frac{1}{2}$ ft. before the end is stopped. And it is the one that bears the bunch if any is to be allowed at that spur. The second growth, which is the nearest to the rod, is pinched back when three or four leaves have formed. Side-shoots produced from these leaf axils are likewise stopped when they have produced two or three leaves only, and so on. My idea is that, should the new growth snap off when being tied down, the chances are that it will do so above the reserve one, so leaving that to take its place if necessary.

If that method of allowing two growths is followed, then when it is time to prune in winter, first of all the growth farthest from the rod should be shortened—this is the one which was allowed to grow $2\frac{1}{2}$ ft. long and possibly bear fruit—back to the reserved growth that is nearest the rod, and which was kept pinched back during the season. This reserve growth is then pruned back to the rod, leaving two visible eyes from which next year's shoots will start in spring (see Fig. 10).

Horizontal Rods

Training vines to produce fruits from rods that are trained horizontally along wires under the roof is very simple, but it involves slightly different techniques to those for single vertical rods. Instead of just one new stem from the stump, the requisite number of rods start from it, like blackberry brambles from the root, and

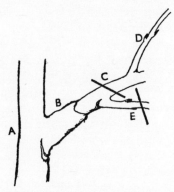

Fig. 10. Where to prune when two buds instead of one are retained
on a shoot growing from a spur
Key: A, main rod; B, permanent spur; C, part of shoot remaining
from previous winter, from which two new growths grew during
summer; D, one growth allowed to extend and possibly bear fruit;
E, second shoot stopped during the summer now becomes the base
of next year's shoots

these are curved and tied to the trellis in tiers. If the root is outdoors, the stump is lengthened until its end ejects into the house,
from where the requisite number of rods are encouraged to grow.

The initial training is much the same as for vertical rods. The
necessary removal of unwanted shoots by rubbing them off while
quite small is done, and also the tenuous growths are moderately
shortened back, especially if they are rather weak, each winter,
until they are considered strong enough to be permanent rods
throughout the length of the house.

Another important point to remember is that all spurs should
be formed along the tops of the rods, and not on opposite sides as
for vertical ones. These rods are spaced 2 ft. apart, one above the
other in tiers. Wires are spaced a foot apart, so having blank ones
between each pair of rods. The wires should be as far as possible
from the glass up to 18 in., and not less than 10 in.

The spurs along the tops of the rods should be spaced, as
nearly as possible, about a foot apart. From each will grow one or
more shoots, just as they do on the vertical rods. These growths
are tied to the blank wires and are stopped when they have
attained 2 ft. which is, of course, the distance up to the rod
immediately above (see Fig. 11).

The very healthy vines can be planned to produce one bunch of grapes on each spur in alternate years. Therefore, each bunch is given a space 4 sq. ft., being 2 ft. wide, and high. That is perfection seldom attained. The crop not only exhausts the vine as a whole, but also each spur from which the bunches come are best when only allowed to crop once every two years—or sometimes three.

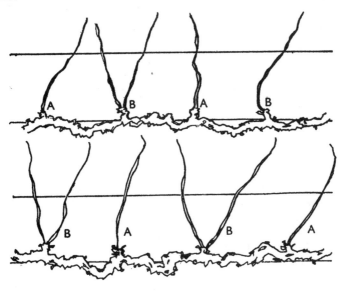

FIG. 11. Vine rods grown on the horizontal system. All the spurs are on the upper sides of the rods. The fruit is borne on alternate spurs each year, on A one year, B the second year, and A again the following year. Note the method of training with cross wires

Long Rod System

While those two forms of training are the main ones, and can be employed for practically every position, even in pots, there are other systems beloved by some specialists that are frequently discussed. One such is the 'Long Rod System'.

It is a very useful system to know. The biggest bunches come from that method of training. Broadly speaking, it can be likened to the usual way of growing ramblers, whereas the permanent rod system is comparable to that for climbing roses.

The simple form is for the young rod, more often referred to as a cane, to grow from the base to the top of the house until it reaches the top, and then it is tipped. At the end of the year any side-shoots on it are shortened back to eyes. At the same time, the previous year's cane, or stem, produces lateral growths from top to bottom, some of which are allowed to bear fruit, and the others stopped appropriately to cover the area with good foliage. Every year this is then removed while the young cane is grown up alongside it.

But it is not always as straightforward as that. A young cane will not grow robustly enough throughout its length in one season, to be able to bear a crop all along its length in the next. So, there is a triplicate method of growing the rods. We have three vertical stems growing from the stump. One is three years old, the next two, and the youngest just one. The oldest one bears bunches on the top half, after which it is completely cut away. The two year old bears bunches on the lower half only, having its top half cut off the winter before. While bearing those bunches it also produced the upper new stem to the top. In its third year, as already stated, it produces bunches at top, but the bottom half is denied that pleasure, being there merely to feed the top through its system. The one year old grows up beside the other two during the summer, and then in winter is shortened by half so that in its second year it bears a crop on the lower half that is left.

Now, for a small house, or a pot, it is possible and can well be the best thing to grow vines by a shortening of the Long Rod System. A new stem is allowed to grow from the base every season. It is shortened to whatever length is best in the winter, and after allowing it to fruit from the side growths in the next summer, it is cut completely away, and replaced with another new one that has grown in the meantime. Thus only the proper length is allowed to mature each year, removing the ends that would have overcrowded the position, and yet the vine is allowed to make fresh considerable growth every season. This will produce very large bunches. It is the way the old cultivators obtained their record breakers.

Quite often, if old vines have produced lengthy spurs on aged

58

rods, it will pay to encourage the production of new stems from below, getting them firm and strong, and then removing the old ones close to the stump. This will rejuvenate the whole appearance. An old axiom is that best grapes grow on young wood that is on old roots. To which I add, if old roots are healthy.

There are other systems, but I do not wish to belabour this any further. Once the principles are grasped, all sorts of things can be done to a long-suffering vine. But you must understand what you are doing. You link basic knowledge with a degree of intuition.

Many times in this chapter the word 'growth' has been used when it should strictly be 'lateral' in the jargon of the indoor gardener. I really do not like the word, although it is more correct. But my chief concern is to try to make descriptions as explicit as possible.

5–The Year's Attentions

We have considered the ideal type of vinery, the soil, the planting and the initial training of the vine in various forms. Now we will run through the usual routine of cultivations, throughout the year, of an established vinery.

As previously stated, the form of cultivation I advocate for the small garden greenhouse is rather different to that which was practised in large gardens where there were elaborate heating systems. Therefore, the form of cultivation advocated here is simpler than was necessary in the past.

Let us look at the varying attentions needed season by season, rather than month by month. If we do it by a monthly calendar it will not work out satisfactorily, for the reason that what is good for one vine in February, say, is out of the question for another.

When vines are not allowed sufficient cold in winter they start to grow much earlier, consequently, just when there are early spring fluctuations of weather, as there invariably are, these need delicate attention regarding temperatures and ventilations.

Late starting vines are easier to grow than those forced, be it ever so slightly. Light also plays an important part in the vine's growing life, and if it has to grow when there are too many hours of darkness all sorts of bothers are exacerbated.

Winter

So, always give the vines a good winter rest. While it may be wise to keep frosts from young planting canes, the established plants can take all the cold imaginable. But this should be consistent, right from the beginning once they have attained fruiting size. It is bad to try to force them one year and then retard them the next. Like almost everything else, vines are plants of habit, and if stimulated into growth one year, may wish to repeat this the next season.

Once the leaves have fallen the ventilators should be opened as

60

far as possible. If there are water pipes, empty them. Keep the ventilators open day and night until late February, or March. Only when there are signs that the plants want to grow again should they be 'started' once more, and then we give them the 'spring' treatment (see page 62).

During this dormant period the winter pruning should be completed. The earlier this is the better. The laterals are cut off from the rods close to the spurs, which are really the swollen basal eyes or buds of previous laterals.

Here I must reiterate, and elaborate upon this subject, first described in the previous chapter. I mentioned cutting back to two eyes instead of one so that there are two future laterals from the same spur, in case one was knocked off. Actually, it is difficult to be so precise about this. What is done is to leave visible eyes beyond the knobbly spur not more than an inch or so, and make the cut so that the last eye retained on the spur is from $\frac{1}{4}$—$\frac{1}{2}$ in. from where the cut is made.

But when pruning, we must remember that good bunches of fruit are only produced on healthy, well-formed laterals and such laterals can only grow from good eyes. Therefore, in order to strengthen the growths from a weak eye, it is shortened back fairly hard, and no fruit is allowed to grow from that during the next season.

In the case of the laterals growing along the tops of horizontal vines, the old gardeners managed to alternate the bunches so that each lateral eye only produced fruit every other year, instead of each year. They were akin to biennial bearing in apple trees.

Whether upright or horizontal, the pruning should be done before the New Year. If left later there may be 'bleeding' at all the spurs, and particularly at the extreme end of the rod. This is an exudation of sap, which is difficult to check once it gets going. It does not kill the vine but it does 'sap' its vitality. If pruning is late, a safeguard is to seal the cut by applying Bentley's Styptic, or shellac, or even furniture polish.

Once pruned you lower the rod from its support, rub off all the rough bark with your hands, taking care not to injure the eyes, and then spray with a weak solution (5 per cent) of tar oil.

At one time we used to scrape off all the bark, then sponge the rods with Gishurst Compound. In addition, all the surrounds were scrubbed with clean water and any brickwork whitewashed.

While giving the vinery a spring clean is a good thing, it is no longer deemed necessary to continue the scraping ritual.

After spraying, the rods, if upright ones, should not be put back against the wires, but be left to dangle horizontally along the back of the vinery, suspending them by string so that they are just above the ground. This is done to check the flow of sap when it starts. Pruned vines are inclined to produce strong shoots at the ends of the rods, at the expense of the ones nearer ground unless this precaution is taken.

The other attention in winter is to refreshen the soil borders. First of all, about 2 in. of the surface is scraped off and taken away. Then a new mulch of chopped loam, to which is added some well decayed manure, is given. The mulch can be enriched with bonemeal, and the vine also likes potash. An alternative is to obtain a special proprietary Vine Border Compound. At least one firm, Bentley's (see Appendix), can still supply it.

During this rest period we need not give much water and surely not dribs and drabs. Nevertheless, the borders should never be allowed to become really dry. If in doubt, give a thorough soaking and then wait until it becomes apparently necessary to repeat this.

Never worry about the frost. The colder it is during the worst days of winter the longer the vines will take to start growing in the spring. It is when they start to grow too early they can go wrong. For once they do, it is spring for them, and we must give them the awakening treatment.

Spring

Spring generally starts in March or, in late years, early April, when there are apparent signs that the eyes of the vine are swelling. When this occurs, the ventilators are closed. The borders are given a good watering, if they need it, and we try to maintain an equable temperature of about 45° F. (7° C.) by night and 50° F. (10° C.) by day. If an automatic electric fan heater is available, its thermostat is set at 45° F. (7° C.). In some models the fan works continuously whether or not heat is being emitted. This is good.

When the inside temperature rises above 50° F. (10° C.) the top ventilators (not the side or front ones) are opened to enable the air to interchange with the colder outdoors, but they are shut down again in early afternoon. On sunny days, the rods are sprayed with a fine nozzled syringe. But at other times, especially dull days, care is taken to see that there is no free moisture about.

After a few weeks the eyes definitely start sending out small shoots. The temperature is gradually increased so that there is no ventilation given before the thermometer reading is 55° F. (13° C.). But it should be given at that degree. If shoots are forced by high day temperatures, they become drawn and weak and may be damaged by cold nights. The thermostat is likewise adjusted to stop emitting heat at 55° F. (13° C.).

Sometime in April, it may be early or late, according to the weather and the respective varieties, the shoots will start growing in earnest, and when about 2 in. long, the upright rods—when that is the system—can be fixed in position under the roof, to the wire trellis. Tie firmly but not too tightly, using soft, untarred fillis twine.

If the weather is fine and sunny, syringe the vines and the interior in the early morning and early afternoon. But not in the late afternoon. On foggy and dull days do not give any surface moisture.

This is rather a tricky time. Nevertheless, if not allowed to become too warm by day, or cold at night, all will be well. If there is an electric fan heater which continues to disturb the air whether or not the heat is above the thermostat level of 55° F. (13° C.), it is a wonderful aid.

Shoots continue to grow steadily, in order to reach the light. These will soon have to be pulled back so that they can be tied to the wires. This must be done gradually or they will snap off. If good wide raffia is used, and looped over the shoots, and tightened up from day to day they will surely be brought to the horizontal position. This is best done in the evenings when they are most pliable.

Along the stems will arrive embryo bunches. As the shoots, now becoming laterals, are pulled down to the trellis, the bunches will dangle down below the wires. For the moment they are all allowed to grow, but any tendrils that form along the stems are pinched off.

Some of the spurs will have a number of shoots or laterals growing from them. Others will only have one. The best one is pulled back down to the trellis, as just described, and as far as possible have it growing at right-angles from the spur, either to the right or the left of the rod, as the case may be.

The best laterals should be left to grow for a while, but the rest, if any, can have their tips pinched out when two or three leaves have formed, to stop them spreading further.

When the one which is being allowed to grow and bear the bunch has formed four or five leaves beyond the bunch, the growing tip can be pinched out too. And also laterals bearing no fruit on other spurs are likewise stopped when about 2 ft. long.

From the laterals will come side-shoots, or 'sub-laterals', which are also pinched back when they have formed two leaves. Always, as far as possible, do this when the last leaf is about the size of a shilling, pinching close back to it, so that this forms the extremity.

But do use discretion about all this, and not work to rule-of-thumb. What you are striving to achieve is a canopy of good healthy foliage that is not overcrowded. We must allow for leaves to develop all through the season. There must be a good spread, but not too much. It does much harm to allow a thicket of growth to develop and then thin it drastically.

Now the day and night temperatures will increase. Set the thermostat at 60° F. (16° C.) and open the day ventilators at 70° F. (21° C.). More moisture by spraying and damping down can be given if the atmosphere is drying. More ventilation can be given at the top, and if it is warm and sultry, the lower ventilators can also be opened.

Summer

For our purposes summer begins when the bunches come into flower. This may be in May or early June. At this time we keep them rather dryish, but it does them good to spray in the afternoon or early evening. Pollen will spread about when dry, but it is better if it has the equivalent of rain or moisture between times.

In the early morning, the rods are tapped sharply to cause the flower caps to drop. Then, about noon, if you draw your hand down over each bunch in a caressing manner you will distribute pollen, and by going from bunch to bunch and rod to rod, carry it from flower to flower. This is done daily for almost a week.

But not all these bunches are allowed to grow. By this time it

3. This is a first-class lean-to peach house (by kind permission of G. F. Strawson & Son, Horley, Surrey).

4. Interior of a peach house; note the front trellis curved over to allow light to reach the wall (*by kind permission of G. F. Strawson & Son*).

will be easy to see which are going to be good, and almost half of the existing bunches are pinched off, the best ones being left.

However, once fruitlets are seen to be forming upon those left, syringeing is done more often, and a 'growing' atmosphere encouraged, but always some ventilation must be given so that there is little or no condensation.

If nights are cold, keep thermostat at 60° F. (16° C.) and if there is an automatic ventilator opener at the top, also set that similarly. It does not matter if the sun raises the temperature considerably by day. But when it does, allow plenty of ventilation above and below. If there is a cold wind, take care to avoid draughts by closing inflow apertures. The best judge is your own feelings. If the atmosphere is good for you, it is good for the vines.

Old gardeners always state that the atmosphere should be 'buoyant'. This is difficult to describe intelligently. For me it is my feelings, but my feelings may not be similar to people who live in air-conditioned homes. The vinery should not feel muggy, or close. There should be a sense of semi-moist air that circulates lightly. Not violently, nor rapidly, from cold to warmth that escapes too quickly at the top. So much depends upon the weather and the direction of the winds.

After a while the small berries will become the size of marrow-fat peas. It is then time to make the first thinning. In some varieties, such as 'Black Hamburgh' and 'Foster's Seedling', the fruits will be much of a muchness. In others, it is possible for there to be a proportion that do not swell. These are imperfectly pollinated and should be snipped off with a special pair of vinery scissors.

Thinning grapes is rather a trying operation, involving a degree of judgement much determined by the variety of grape. For example, 'Gros Colman' has very large round berries, on medium, rather compact bunches. The eventual swelling room needed by each one has to be anticipated and allowed for. 'Foster's Seedling' has oval berries which need less room in the bunch itself. 'Black Hamburgh' has berries between these two, being slightly oval and large. The inner ones within the bunch should always be removed and always leave the extremities, then discreetly thin out the 'face' berries.

At this time a fillip of fertiliser is helpful. There are proprietary

E   65

vine foods, such as Thompson's or Bentley's, or dried blood can be used. Just for a day or two after this, beware of any faintest smells from the fertiliser, and if they do, open the top ventilator a little more until they have ceased.

After this, moisture is spread around more freely, so obtaining more humidity. But a problem here is that, if there is moisture upon the foliage and fruitlets when the early morning sun warms up the house too sharply, there will be scorching. As far as possible, I like to do the last damping down about tea-time so that it evaporates during the next few hours before the coldness of night.

Just a little ventilation at night will do much to minimise this bother. And if the fan is working, while the thermostat is set at 60° F. (16° C.), it will be ideal.

We must remember that where the vines grow best in the open air, such as the plains between Baalbek and Beirut, where incidentally I once sat among the vines to taste the grapes, it is cold by night and very warm by day.

When about half grown there will seem to be no further swelling of the berries. They are just now more concerned with the stones inside them than the flesh. Take care not to force them unduly, just giving them the warmth of sunshine, the humidity, and the ventilation when the temperature is around 70° F. (21° C.) inside.

Throughout the period, ensure that water is given to the border when wanted. And the continuously growing foliage will need stopping here and there to keep the canopy fairly moderate, the individual leaves having just enough space.

Then will come a renewed swelling of the berries. This is a good time for a second application of fertiliser, taking the precaution mentioned previously concerning possible fumes.

If the thinning of the grapes when they were as large as marrowfat peas is proving to have been insufficient, it may be possible to correct this now. But this cannot be overdone, as it is so easy to damage those left by touching them. The extended shoulders of the bunches can be helped by suspending them to the wires by pieces of raffia being passed through the stems and stalks and looped up. This stops the berries on the shoulders pressing down upon those of the main bunch.

Autumn

We now come to the most important quarter of the year, if the crop is the chief reason for growing. When the black varieties show definite signs of changing colour, or the white ones become paler, and somewhat opalescent, it is time to give them all the light and air that is possible without creating a cold draught. Watch the way the wind blows, and when not dangerous, open the lower and top ventilators. And when nights are warmer, which is usual at this season, some ventilation can be kept on all the time.

The foliage shields the bunches from the bright sunshine, but glimpses of the sun through the leaves will be helpful. Old gardeners make a fetish of stating emphatically that white varieties should have more light than dark ones, but there are more important points to emphasise. Nevertheless, if there are any leaves or shoots giving too much shade they are pinched off.

We always pinch off green growth rather than cut it with knives or secateurs. There is less abrasion and hardly any bleeding.

Some grapes normally start the colouring process in July. Some start in late August or September. Some take a long time to ripen. 'Hamburgh' needs about six weeks. Muscats need nine. 'Gros Colmar' needs still more and continues to swell once colouring starts.

At this stage it is wrong to withhold watering or moisture, but, on the other hand, it should not be given so freely as before. On warm, sunny, late summer days a nice damp down will assist ripening. At the same time, to reiterate, all the ventilation possible will be helpful. The bottom ventilators and the top can be extended fully. And at night, unless there is an unusual chilliness, they can be left partly open.

The very late varieties, such as 'Gros Colmar', will, if the border is moist, need no damping down towards the ripening period. The ventilators should be kept partly open at night, and opened fully on very warm days. The fan heater, if any, can be 60° F. (16° C.) and kept running, the moving air being just right. If other plants like chrysanthemums are brought into the house at this time of year this air-fan will do them good too.

The last problem is when to gather the crop. Generally, the longer left, within reason, the better the flavour and the more

67

sweetness. While they are ripening always keep the border watered, but do not damp down in any way, and keep the ventilators open.

If there is a surplus to be stored, the best way to do it is to cut the bunches with a reasonable length of the old lateral stem intact, and insert the basal end of this in a bottle of soft water, placing the bottle where it can be fixed at an angle so that the bunch is suspended clear of its side. The building should be airy, cool and frostproof. The garage is quite a good place.

Do not prune the vine again until all the leaves have fallen. It is then where we started the annual round at the beginning of this chapter.

Heated Vineries

This exercise has been solely concerned with unheated greenhouses, or, preferably, those helped by an electric heater.

The methods described may be disputed by the old traditionalists, whose ideas involved large cumbersome collections of hot-water pipes. I have had vineries myself where the pipes were in six pairs. That number ensured an equable heat that was neither too dry nor scorching.

During the war they had to be removed. The outcome was that the one vine left received hardly any artificial warmth, survived, and gave better crops than ever before.

These pipes are necessary for early cropping, but they cannot supply light, and it is a very skilled and painstaking job to obtain crops by this means. One of the problems, for instance, is ensuring that the growing shoots in spring break evenly. Some on the rods will be 6 in. or more long, when others are just swelling. To try to rectify matters, the rods were taken down from the trellis and suspended horizontally, as described earlier. Another method was to warm the pipes, keep the house warm, and use plenty of moisture to give a close, humid atmosphere, it being thought that this would force the rods. In my opinion, the roots were the cause of the trouble, they not being equal to the pressure being brought upon them by the artificial heat.

If heat is used, much the same programme as described in this chapter will bring results. It is just a matter of putting the seasonal operations forward. Under those circumstances, summer can well be in spring.

Another reason for delayed natural starting, after the winter exposure, is in the care of a vine, all of whose roots are outdoors, and especially when they have a free run. It is only reasonable to assume that, where the one part is cool, while the other is forced by artificial heat, there are bound to be complications. Heated houses, especially those started off too early, are most affected with the bothers and troubles reviewed in the next chapter.

Of course, for heated houses the winter calendar is brought forward. Just when the vines are still resting in the ordinary way, they are stimulated into growth, which is often erratic, and the same conditions must be maintained, much as are needed for the cooler grown vines. It is difficult, and that is why growing grapes in heat has been regarded as a task for specialists.

If this chapter has given the impression that vines are difficult, it is a wrong one. They do need the right treatment, but no more than is necessary for other plants. It has taken considerable length to explain these methods, but that is mainly to try to impart a sense of understanding. If the gist of the techniques is grasped, the rest comes with experience and a 'feeling' that guides the grower in his actions.

6—Vine Afflictions

As with all other sorts of vegetation, vines have their afflictions, although I contend that they are not as numerous as those of roses, nor so obstinate as those of indoor carnations. They can be put into the three categories of functional disorders, insect pests, and diseases closely connected with fungi.

Functional Disorders

Shanking

This is quite a common ailment. It starts at the time when the grower thinks there is going to be a fine crop. Some of the berries at the tips of the bunches develop spots, that then begin to wither, and then the stalks and stems of these berries turn a rusty colour. The fruits are extremely bitter.

The trouble is attributed to functional disorders. If the roots are suffering from rot, or have grown extensively in search of moisture and food, when given a free run, and the weather and conditions generally then make it impossible for them to find it, shanking becomes serious. Little can be done about it, except to snip off the affected parts.

If the border is inside, a too light soil which drains out too quickly, or at the other extreme, one that has been too compact and made greasy by topdressings, will cause the roots to shrink, or go down to the foundations. Under these circumstances, the old professionals used to adopt a major operation.

They lifted all the roots during the rest period, took the soil away, and then replanted them in a new compost. This involved a great deal of labour and materials, but being carried out in the winter time the cost was of secondary importance.

Most often, the roots, which were carefully removed, and wrapped and put aside temporarily while the work proceeded, were bereft of fibrous rootlets. So when they were replanted, notches were made in the stem of these main roots from which it was firmly believed that new fibrous roots would come. They usually did. Another practice was to graft the scions of varieties prone to shanking upon rootstocks of those that rarely suffer from the trouble.

In two vineries, where we had muscats with outdoor root runs, we were much worried with shanking. On the other hand, we had the 'Foster's Seedling' with all its roots inside, growing in unchanged soil for over 30 years. It bore good crops that never shanked. The appropriate feeds kept it going.

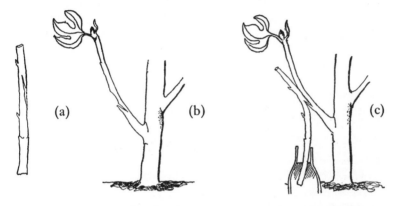

FIG. 12. (a) Shows stages in preparing the scion of a vine for a bottle graft
(b) Shows the stock and a suitable shoot for receiving the scion
(c) Shows the scion fitted to the stock before binding with tape

There are three ways of grafting or budding. One is to insert an eye in the rod just above the ground. Another is to put a retarded scion on the top of a vine root, where the top had been cut off just above ground level. This form of saddle grafting is comparatively easy, but care has to be taken to see that there is no bleeding, and also, soil should be heaped over the graft. All these practices involve skill and care and the reader is advised to study a specialist work such as *The Grafter's Handbook*, by R. J. Garner. However, bottle-grafting is probably the best and easiest means of changing an established vine from one variety to another. It can be carried out successfully when the recipient vine is just bursting into leaf in spring while the scion that is taken off the other vine is still comparatively dormant.

Needless to say, the vine from which the scion is taken must be healthy. The shoot itself should have formed the previous summer, and have upon it plenty of strong buds suggesting power and strength. A cut is made so that eyes are left at each end, and the graft should be about 18 in. long.

About 8 in. from the top end a crescent of bark and wood is cut out to a length of about 4 in. That done, another incision is made upwards in this crescent, to form a tongue as in Fig. 12 (a).

The shoot growing on the recipient vine should also be a previous summer's growth, possibly near the base of the rod from which it is growing, and should have its end shortened so that it is a few inches taller than where the union is to be made. If possible, this shortening of the long roots should have been made in the dormant season, so avoiding risk of bleeding.

A crescent of 4 in. length is cut out, just as was done with the scion, and then an incision made downwards, so forming a tongue that sticks upwards, as in (b). The two are then dovetailed together, as in (c). They must fit perfectly and care must be taken to see that the cut parts of bark and wood meet precisely. They can then be bound together with binding tape or proper grafting bands (obtainable from Bentley's).

The bottle of water is placed so that it sustains the base of the scion. The shoot on the parent plant above the scion should be allowed to grow until there are signs of a cohesion. This is when the eyes of the scion above the union begin to grow. Then the parent shoot is stopped from growing further, but allowed to retain the leaves it has formed in the meantime.

If the scion takes, it will soon grow. The shoot, or the best, if more than one, should soon attain 6 ft. or so. At this stage all the growth that is above the union is removed, and all the stump that was in the bottle, up to the union on that side. Incidentally, the base should be kept in the bottle until the top is growing quite strongly.

One of the advantages of this form of grafting is that the vine to which the transplant is being given can still be allowed to bear that season's crop on the other shoots. The old is only removed when it is certain that the new can replace it. Therefore, you can experiment without dire consequences. All these three ways involve skill and care, and the reader is advised to find out more about them. It is sufficient here to state that they can be accomplished.

There is no doubt that shanking often occurs when the crop is too heavy in proportion to the foliage. It is when pinching-back is overdone and there are many bunches that it most frequently occurs, especially with white grapes, which are said to need more light. Obviously, the thing to do is have fewer bunches and allow a little more foliage.

Grapes can be spoilt by over-feeding. And too heavy mulchings. Chilly watering, erratic applications and constant sudden changes of temperature can all contribute to vine bothers, including shanking.

Some have tried to correct the soil by giving lime, and a little sulphate of iron. It is possible to get a fungicide compound, such as Bentley's, which is dug into the border in spring. This has been done successfully when the situation is not desperate.

Of functional disorders that can occur the commonest is sunscald, allied with grapes splitting. These two are most often due to too scanty foliage, lack of ventilation, and stagnant humidity in the ripening stage, and an excess of water at the roots. If borders are outside and autumn rains are heavy, it may be worth while placing a shelter over the bed to ward much of it off. Some varieties are more prone than others, 'Madresfield Court' having a bad reputation in this respect.

Aerial roots are sometimes produced on the stems of vines that also produce really heavy crops of first-class bunches. While this state of affairs is not to be encouraged, for it undoubtedly means a shorter life for the plants, it does indicate the vitality of the vine and its desire to live at all costs. It occurs when the air is charged with moisture and contains ammoniacal vapours and suchlike. It also means that the proper roots are unlikely to be functioning satisfactorily, through bad soil, or not getting good food. Do not force such vines too much, give more ventilation, apply fertilisers if the plants are healthy, and in extremity, change the soil.

There is a complaint known as dropsy, which takes the form of pimples on the underside of the leaves. It happens when the vinery is kept too close, and is caused by a lack of balance between the intake and output of moisture. When the foliage is too drastically reduced the bother is likely to occur. It is not a disease and can only be corrected by good management.

Scorching of the leaves has been mentioned in previous chapters. When they are healthy, the leaves have a nice dewy appearance, especially in the early morning. It is there when the night has not been too warm, but the damage is done when the sun shines brightly and there is not enough ventilation for this dew to disperse before becoming heated. The answer is to make it possible for the moisture to vanish before the sun warms the leaves. The moisture should disappear steadily rather than by a sudden and rash opening of the ventilators. The thermostatically controlled ventilator, set at 50° F. (10° C.), is the answer, or just a little air left on all night, or one can get up very early in the morning and open the ventilators slightly at first, increasing as the temperature rises.

Diseases

Mildew

Powdery mildew affects both indoor and outdoor vines and forms a white covering all over the leaves, flowers and fruits. It will turn berries rotten and unpleasant. In my young days it was the bugbear of the indoor grape producer, and all sorts of desperate treatments were made to arrest it. The usual one was to mix flowers of sulphur in milk and paint the solution on to the hot-water pipes so that the sulphur evaporated into the air. Sulphur in one form or another has always been regarded as the cure for moulds and mildews in all shapes and forms, and it is undoubtedly a good antidote. But it can also harm the subjects it is supposed to protect.

In recent years, dinocap has been proven a safer and surer control. It is often sold under the trade name of Karathane, several firms formulating it for garden use. It is available as a smoke, i.e. a small cone which is set alight to give off a vapour, or it can be used as a liquid wash, being obtainable also as a wettable powder.

Dinocap (or Karathane) does not stain or harm the grapes, provided that it is applied when the temperature is not too high. Evening is the best time. It is also effective upon other crops like chrysanthemums, although there are one or two varieties of these that can be damaged.

The main reasons for the appearance of mildew are overcrowded foliage, insufficient ventilation, too dry an atmosphere, and inconsiderate fluctuations in temperature. There are other forms of mildew that rarely appear on vines, such as the continental one that attacks the underside of the leaves. I have never met them.

Grey Mould (*Botrytis cinerea*)

This can be a nuisance in unheated houses. However, if a fan heater is used it will not be troublesome. It is caused by keeping the ventilators shut so that there is a damp close atmosphere. It is similar to that which occurs outdoors on strawberries. If this is the only trouble, without powdery mildew being present, I would try captan, which should not be mixed with sulphur or dinocap.

Pests

Red Spider Mite

The worst problem of the vinery that is too dry is red spider mite. It is not so prevalent in large vineries as in smaller ones because the atmosphere can be kept more evenly charged with the moisture that the red spider does not like. Its presence is indicated by the dirty, discoloured and dejected-looking leaves that are plastered with almost invisible eggs, and often a fine web, particularly on the underside. It is barely visible without a hand lens.

The one sure chemical that will eradicate the pest is azobenzene. It has to be applied carefully, one way being by fumigating smokes. Several firms manufacture these and they are packed in sizes to suit the greenhouse cubic capacity, which should always be carefully checked.

Another control is by electric aerosols. These are heated cups kept at a cool, even temperature, that emit continuous vapour into the atmosphere, so finely that it does no harm to the user but does keep the greenhouse free of pests. There are various formulas for other insects, such as white flies, aphis, etc., the charges being interchangeable for the same dispenser. I have found this form of control of insect and fungal troubles the most economical, the most effective, and the easiest way of dealing with all of them.

However, where these cannot be applied, for various reasons, there are two organo-phosphorous chemicals that will now most effectively dispose of red spider. This group of chemicals does contain among it some very dangerous formulas, but of the two that are comparatively harmless, malathion will only affect those who are allergic to phosphorus. Several companies manufacture it in branded packets. The other is diazinon, used as an aerosol or liquid. Both completely break down within a short time, leaving no trace. Of the two I prefer malathion. If the warnings and instructions of the manufacturers are read and heeded, such insecticides are safer to use than old-fashioned poisons such as nicotine, and are non-poisonous after a few hours.

Vine Louse (Phylloxera)

This is the much publicised pest that attacks vine roots and at one time ravaged continental vineyards. Although it came from America, it does not attack American rootstocks as much as those of European origin. In recent times it has, happily, become rarer than rabies is among our dogs. It forms galls on the roots, much like a mild attack of clubroot on cabbage plants. The louse also forms smaller galls on the leaves, from which new wingless insects emerge, which then work their way down to the roots. This is a notifiable pest, like the Colorado Beetle, and just as seriously important, and as unlikely to occur. If suspicious, the best procedure is to apply to the Horticultural Adviser of your local County Council, who will be able to help you.

Vine Weevil

Although this pest is mostly called the Vine Weevil it will eat many other plants, such as stonecrops, houseleeks, ferns, begonias, cyclamen and primulas (Royal Horticultural Society's *Dictionary of Gardening*). The adults are about one-third of an inch long, of a dull black colour and have yellow specks on them. They feed upon leaves at night and hide during the day. Once established they are difficult to eradicate.

Malathion and similar organo-phosphorous dispersible insecticides are not so good for dealing with them, as they can escape and then return when the potency has gone. Instead, we must find a more persistent insecticide, but one that is not as permanent as some of the organo-chlorines. 'Sevin Dust' is one of the best available at the present time.

The old way was to lay pieces of cloth under the vines in the daytime, and then at night go into the vinery and shake the rods so that the weevils fell down into them. You had to be very alert.

I am not an enthusiast about chemicals, but do prefer them to many of the old poisons such as arsenic, red lead, nicotine and mercury, which were far more dangerous and much less selective.

Mealy-bug

When mealy-bug infects a vinery it spoils everything, and was once a scourge difficult to clear. It is itself red-coloured, but made prominent by a white, woolly sticky substance that is extremely unpleasant. It is unmistakable.

One way I have cleared it is to open all the ventilators and the door in winter, when very frosty, and spray all the surface of the building and the vines with clear water. All becomes encased in fine ice that kills the pest.

Routine spraying with tar oil in winter is also helpful, but if made too strong it will damage, or kill the eyes of the rods. If there is a suggestion of its being present in spring, I make two sprayings of malathion diluted to manufacturer's instructions. With freezing, followed by malathion, in almost every case, you will find no more mealy-bug.

For those who are allergic to malathion, a petroleum oil insectide can be used. But for those who are not, malathion is more effective and it completely evaporates after four days. If sprayed in the evening, the ventilators should be opened next day to clear the atmosphere. Do not stay with it unnecessarily.

Thrips

There are a number of thrips that attack vines, the commonest being that invisible creature whose whereabouts can be detected by a dark juice upon the lower parts of the leaves. These pests are also found upon many other greenhouse occupants, such as azaleas, and are often carried into the vinery upon such plants. Like red spider mite, they love rather dry conditions. Malathion will clear them.

Scale Insects

These are much in the same order as mealy-bug, and crawl around when young, to settle later permanently upon the stems of plants. They can often be seen on asparagus fern. Malathion is the surest insecticide to clear these; you can also struggle with a nicotine wash.

Other possible pests are aphids and moths, the eggs of which can be destroyed by the mild tar oil wash (5 per cent) in the middle of winter when the vines are dormant, and a further routine malathion spray in early summer.

Ants can be a nuisance in any greenhouse, chiefly by carrying aphids and so on from plant to plant. When they are seen the best antidote is one of the proprietary ant baits.

While this list of fungal and insect pests seems rather formidable, it should be realised that very few are probable in a good vinery, and some are only very remote possibilities.

The first trouble dealt with in this chapter was shanking. To me it is the worst bother of all because it only comes when there is the promise of reward for the whole year's work. It is avoided by having the Sweetwater varieties, and by heeding all the not too difficult but moderate needs that the most wonderful of all fruits expect.

PART TWO
Peaches, Nectarines, Figs and Trees in Pots

7—Peaches and Nectarines: Border Preparation

Peaches and nectarines are the finest and most adaptable fruits to grow in greenhouses of every description, and particularly those small structures seen in gardens that are often lying idle, having originally been put to less practical uses.

There is no need to worry about heating apparatus. Although these fruits can be forced into earlier cropping when houses are fitted with hot-water pipes, or air ducts, or electrical equipment, it is really better to have no heat at all than too much. Probably the best aid, if any, as for grapes, is a small turbine electric heater that can be turned on in the spring when frosts prevail, or in autumn if the crop is late, to assist ripening. Even then, the thermostat should be set at about 45° F. (7° C.) so that there is never too close a temperature.

Peaches will grow outdoors, as everyone knows, but there are the hazards that do not arise with the protection of glass. One can rely upon crops every year indoors. There is no bother with adverse weather, and difficult troubles like peach leaf curl, while the fruits are less likely to be attacked by rodents. There are, however, some pests we have to contend with in greenhouses, but these are controllable and are due, in most cases, to faulty cultivation.

I contend that peaches and nectarines grown under glass possess qualities unsurpassed by any cultivated in the open in any country of the world. Peaches are large, juicy, tender and have flavour such as one cannot obtain from orchard-grown trees. They are kept on the trees in the greenhouses until they ripen. Those one buys are gathered long before ripeness, and soften, rather than mature in transit. If one can grow first-class peaches, and nectarines, they will be enjoyed to an extent never experienced before.

F

Growing peaches and nectarines is just as easy, or as difficult as you wish to make the pastime. The routine is not so much rule-of-thumb as an ability to understand what the trees want and provide their needs. However, there are techniques to learn. At various times of year we must, of course, prune, train, spray, feed, and ventilate, according to the weather, and stage of growth. It is not difficult, although this list may seem forbidding.

The best-ever greenhouse crops were tended by country lads who learned their job very quickly. What they could do you should do better, considering the modern aids and facilities, especially when compared with the old crude conditions. In fact, it is possible to eliminate many of the old chores by automation.

Supports

Although these fruits can be adapted to all sorts of conditions, they must have suitable borders for the roots to grow in, and wire trellises have to be fitted to which the trees can be trained. And there should be a fairly generous ventilation system. The latter necessity is hardly ever a serious problem, for greenhouses of every class and type are fitted with sashes that can be regulated.

The wire trellises are sometimes fitted, but more often not. Generally, a local blacksmith can and will make angle irons that can be fixed to the ends of the houses, inside, and into which holes have been drilled through which the wires can be inserted. The first horizontal wire should be about 18 in. off ground level, and the rest spaced about 8 in. apart up to the apex of the roof. Thus there are from 10–15 wires from bottom to top, these being about a foot from the glass. They are generally fixed so that the sharp angle where the roof slants from the upright walls, is streamlined, to form a gentle curve.

Border Preparation

Probably the biggest job is to prepare the borders for the roots. In some soils, where there is natural drainage, a lot of work is not essential. If the locality is one where stone fruits will grow without bother, and the soil in the borders inside the house is of the same calibre, there is not much to do really. Alas, the natural conditions for peaches and nectarines are not always found, therefore it becomes a question of whether it is worth while making the usual somewhat elaborate preparations. Just because

82

experts in the past have ordained that these elaborations are necessary is no reason why this should be. Although the best fruits have not always come from such unnatural beds they are less likely to come from unprepared ones. What to do should be determined by learning to know what peach trees like and then the conditions deemed most suitable in the circumstances should be supplied.

Drainage

The first essential is drainage. While peaches suffer very much if they are short of water at the roots, they also suffer if the roots are ever in a saturated state.

They also like sunshine. Therefore, the best position for a peach house is in a rather high, sunny position. It can be a lean-to on the sunny side of a wall. Existing small structures can easily be moved. The obvious way to ensure drainage is to build up the border as high as possible. And also to place drainage pipes down below, if they can be fitted. We should, as far as possible, ensure drainage to a depth of almost 3 ft. This can be accomplished in various ways. If there is a convenient main drain which is 3 ft. deep from the border surface, which, I repeat, can often be raised, there is little to do but put in small land-drain pipes through the border, leading to the outlet. If there is no main drain, it may be possible, unless the district is retentively clayey, to make a soakaway by digging a hole outside the house 5 or 6 ft. deep, and filling with clinker, so that the water from the clay pipes disappears easily.

Another way to ensure drainage is to have a sunken path in the greenhouse, with a retaining wall a yard high, built of bricks that have spaces left in the wall, so that surplus water can drain through into the pathway. Water can then be applied until there is a seepage through the wall. In fact, it is a fairly good guide to water requirements, provided it is applied evenly over the whole surface of the border.

Sometimes, instead of the path being a yard below the border surface, there is a conduit, with a grid placed over the top to walk upon, through which can be seen the water that drains out from the brickwork, forming a guide of how much to apply, or cease to apply. When the border is dryish it is soaked until there are signs of it escaping through the wall. The conditions are much as described for a vinery.

83

Soil

The best sort of soil is a fairly heavy loam. Loam is a mixture of clay, sand and humus, such as completely decayed manure. Therefore, a heavy loam contains a considerable amount of clay, but has in it enough sand to allow water to move freely, and enough humus, or decayed manure to provide food. This is quite a common condition for gardens in clay districts, especially where gardeners have cultivated vegetables and flowers over the years. In light sandy localities, the clay is lacking, which is not so favourable for the trees.

The border is generally encased completely inside the house, but where size is extremely small, and the foundations are not deep there is no reason why the roots should not also be allowed to grow out into the open ground as well. However, we must remember that roots are strong, and, unless the foundations are pretty solid, may cause the house to warp, if it is of the wooden type.

The usual quoted size for a peach border is 10 ft. wide, and 2 ft. 9 in. deep, the trees being planted 15 ft. apart. This makes a surface of 150 sq. ft. But, in a greenhouse 12 × 8 ft. I would not hesitate to plant a tree on one side, and have the pathway along the other. It would be far enough away to have narrow shelving on that clear side as well as across the end. I have seen two trees flourishing nicely in a house of this size, one on each side giving a Nissen hut effect through the middle, but they were uncomfortable, and it was equally difficult for the owner to attend to them.

Sometimes gardeners try to make sure of getting wonderful crops by excavating the inside to a depth of 3 ft. or thereabouts, and putting a concrete layer over the bottom to make a concrete floor through which the roots cannot penetrate. A network of small land-drain pipes is then laid to lead surplus water to an outlet, these being held in position and kept open, by a covering of fine clinker, or largish pebbles, or similar materials. Quite often they lead to the holed brick wall made to retain the border, or to support a grid path that is then made at border surface level.

I once had several small houses on sandy well-drained ground where some were prepared for peach and nectarine trees in the manner described in the last paragraph. In another house, no

such preparations were made, but the borders were excavated to
2½ ft. over the whole inside area, and filled with compost without
giving any controlled drainage. In the controlled houses where
drainage was below the path grids, the trees were consistently
good croppers, and easily controllable. Where the drainage was
haphazard, one or two trees did badly, but one has given enormous crops annually for over 30 years, spreading far beyond the
normal room allowed. It was a nectarine of the Pine Apple variety,
which loved the free range above and below ground.

For the borders generally a special loam is used either imported
from Kettering or Surrey, that is chopped up with a spade, rather
than sifted and is laced with other materials in the proportions by
volume of 10 parts loam, 1 part bonemeal, 1 part old mortar
rubble or 'dead' lime, and ½ part wood-ashes, or just a little sulphate of potash. If the loam is very heavy some coarse horticultural sand is added.

Where it is available, the top spit taken off pasture is collected,
and laid in a pile, with the grass laid upside down, and left for a
year or so. It is then ready to chop down to form the main compost. The pile is always made outdoors, where it has all the
benefits of the elements.

Any soil of any sort, especially where no roots are living in it,
is apt to go sour under glass, or in a shed, therefore it is best kept
outdoors until wanted.

Very often, when we build inside borders for fruit trees, and
vines, they are done in sections rather than one complete operation, being added to year by year as the occupants grow. If, for
instance, the maximum sized peach border of 9 ft. is planned in
the first place, only a width of 3 ft. is made up the first year, and
then a further 3 ft. the second year, the remaining 3 ft. being
completed still a year later. Normally, however, borders are
seldom that width. Always, it is a matter of discretion, rather
than dogmatic rulings (as for vines).

If the greenhouse is erected over a part of the garden that has
grown good crops of vegetables, it may not be advisable to go to
all that trouble, especially if the drainage is good, but it may pay
to trench all the soil inside the house to a depth of 2½ ft. and to mix
in a slow-acting fertiliser, mainly of bonemeal, at the rate of 4 or
5 lb. to each square yard of surface. A house 12 × 8 ft. would
thus have mixed in its border, about 3–4 cwt. of slow-acting food.

Here I wish to emphasise that it is wrong to make the borders rich. They should have substance that the trees can draw upon slowly and steadily in the young stages. It is the 'golden mean'. If they grow too rapidly, peach trees do not give the best fruits. If they cannot flourish, through being poverty-stricken, they cannot possibly give good fruits either. There should always be good growing shoots coming every summer, but if they are too soft and lush they will not bear the right crops. This must be remembered when decisions are made about such points as the making of the borders, and of what the bulk of the border should consist.

When making borders, it is never wise to rush the task. If possible, they are best prepared several weeks before planting the trees. They can then settle down naturally rather than be rammed down. If they are to be built in sections, rather than one complete whole, the retaining walls of the sections can be narrow turves piled one above the other, as bricks are in a wall. It is also good to lay turves over the drainage rubble and land-pipes below, always placing the turves grass side downwards.

It is unwise to buy ordinary lawn turves for this purpose. Very often these have been treated with selective weedkillers, which may cause the trees to linger, or even die, without the owner realising what the trouble is. If loam or any border material has to be bought it should invariably be obtained from suppliers who specialise in this form of merchandise (see vines and straw bales, page 43).

8—Choice of Peach and Nectarine Trees

When we buy trees for our greenhouses there are two very important things to consider—the quality of the trees themselves, and the varieties. The amateur may think it a good idea to raise the trees themselves, but responsible gardeners hardly ever attempt to do that. They buy quality.

There are various stages of growth at which trees are offered for sale. They are 'maiden', 'two year old', or 'three year old'. They are also trained in various shapes, chiefly bush, standard, or the fan.

The gardener most often buys two-year-old, fan-trained trees for his greenhouse, if he can, by visiting a reputed nursery and choosing what he considers to be the best. If that is impossible, he orders them from firms that specialise in trained fruit trees, stating clearly and precisely exactly what he wants.

Such trees are only of the best varieties, which we will review later in this chapter. Never have they been raised from stones. It is most inadvisable for anyone to plant a seedling in a greenhouse, for the chances are remote that any good fruit will result. Space is too valuable to take risks, while the time factor matters much.

The trees we should buy are of varieties budded on rootstocks. Those who propagate these discuss and often disagree about rootstocks, for they can be seedling peaches, or almond, or suckers of various wild plums, such as St. Julien A and Brompton. Those who raise bush trees for orchards aver that peach seedlings make better roots for the varieties of peaches that will grow outdoors, more or less, satisfactorily.

I prefer to let the experts wrangle, but to be much more particular about the quality of the trees I buy, rather than concern myself about the source of the roots. These arguments are often due to chance experiences of the growers. There are all sorts of soils that can make those experiences different, and there are good and bad examples of each form and definitely possible unhealthy sources of some rootstocks. Health is far more important than the actual type of roots. Nevertheless, if I am given alternatives, I choose St. Julien A.

Nursery Stock

When one visits a nursery one will, if it is a normal one, be shown fan-trained trees in serried rows, and it will be noted that, although the trees are in alignment, the 'fans' face varying directions making them look awry. This is no accident, but a deliberate bit of work by the propagator, who is more concerned with obtaining an evenly branched fan, and that was the best way to do it on what started as a young bush tree in each case.

Very briefly, I will try to explain how these trees reach the stage in which you see them. We will begin when the nurseryman has obtained his stock of small peach or almond seedlings, or plum suckers or layers and planted them in those rows in the nursery. This he completed in the previous winter. They grew into small bushy trees during spring and summer. They were then budded in July or August, the buds being taken off trees of named varieties, and inserted in the stems of these young bushy trees, one in each stem, a few inches above the ground. Any side-shoots, or suckers, sprouting below the bud, were conscientiously removed before and after budding, but all growths above the bud were allowed to grow unfettered.

After the buds are inserted they do not grow readily at first, but they most often do later. After about a month, the leaves of the buds will drop off when touched, if all is well, but when they are dry and sere and hang on, they have not taken. In that case, another bud is inserted in a different part of each stock. Should that also fail, then the saplings can still be turned to good account by being grafted in the spring.

When winter comes the nurserymen will, if the buds have taken, cut down all the top above that bud, using a very sharp knife so as not to cause injury. Sometimes the stem is cut through several inches above the bud instead, stripping the bit left of any other eyes or growths, so that it merely becomes a blind stump above the inserted bud. This is sometimes used to tie the new shoot to, as it grows in the new spring and summer. This stump has then to be cut off later, just above the bud from which the one strong shoot has since sprung.

At this stage we have the rootstock up to the point where the bud was inserted, and above that the new top, completely replacing the original one.

A Maiden Tree

If you buy a 'maiden', which you are sometimes advised to do, and which are listed in catalogues as such, that is what you are sent. The term 'maiden' is a very old one, being used by propagators for centuries, and has become a normal description for this form of tree, be it peaches or any of the other sorts of fruit grown this way.

When winter returns once more the maiden is again cut down, this time to 6 in. above the bud point, so leaving a stem that consists of half the old rootstock and half the newly imposed variety above it.

In the spring that follows, the part above the bud sends out small branches to form a bushy dwarf tree. These splay out in all directions. It is now the propagator's job to erect a trellis of canes or sticks across the tree at whichever angle he thinks will make it easiest for him to train four or more shoots to, in order to form a fan. He ties back those most suitable, and cuts off neatly those unwanted. So in that succeeding autumn, the rows of trees at their various angles are what you see, when you visit the nursery.

Tree for Quality

Good shaped well-grown trees at this age are known as 'two year old'. Sometimes they are kept for a further year in the nursery and become 'three year old'. They are generally a little more expensive because of that, but they need not be the best to buy. They may have been too weak to sell when younger, or they may have been the rejected surplus of the previous season. It is better to inspect both the two year old and those older to draw comparisons and use discrimination. How to do this is a matter of experience, or learning to distinguish the good from the mediocre.

Never buy a tree that exudes gum from any part of it. See that the shoots, or branches, as I prefer to describe them, are equal and well balanced. The lowest ones, trained to the lowest position should be as strong as, or stronger, than the ones forming the fan above them.

Sometimes the branches are spaced too far apart up the main stem. Within reason, the closer together they are the better. One fault is to have one main stem, with the branches spaced as though they were an espalier. We intend to remove the middle growth, and this can be done more easily if the side branches are close together (see Fig. 13).

FIG. 13. Examples of well, and poorly-shaped young peach and nectarine trees. If the centre growth on the left-hand, well-shaped tree is cut out there will remain good, low branches on each side for future development

Choose those of healthy medium growth, rather than trees that are lush and strong with few buds along the branches. On the other hand, very weak growth shows a weak constitution. The bark of the branches should be reddish-brown rather than pale green, and have a healthy, tough look about it. The bark of the stock below the bud point should be clean and healthy.

The stem of the rootstock should never be thicker than the main stem above the bud point. As far as possible, stock and scion (the part above the bud point) should be equally thick. If there is any difference, the part above should be slightly larger.

There is no such thing as perfection. If it were so, observations like these would be unnecessary. It is almost impossible to get a really truly balanced tree. But having chosen the ones we regard as being the best, we must then do our utmost to train them in the right way afterwards. However, before we deal with that we must also, when buying, consider varieties.

Peaches and/or Nectarines

Here I must distinguish peaches from nectarines, for no other reason than to omit continuously referring to them individually. When dealing with cultivations references to peaches will mean both.

A peach has a rough skin. A nectarine has a smooth one. They are precisely of similar origin, and there is no one I have met who knows the real reason for these variations. Some peaches came from nectarine stones, and vice versa. It does not really matter.

As a general run, peaches are much larger, while nectarines have a more fulsome flavour. Some prefer nectarines to peaches. I think they have a better texture and are richer than peaches.

One point we should remember is that nectarines are not quite so hardy as peaches, for no accountable reason.

There are also other distinctions, especially between peaches, such as some being 'cling-stones'. But I do not think it worth the bother to ponder over this.

Rather, is it better to discuss the most popular varieties, so that the aspiring grower can select according to position and taste.

Although many peaches and nectarines are continuously being raised from stones, most of the named varieties have been cultivated for many years. This is because very few seedlings are equal to these when all things are considered, for not only is their flavour better, but there is a higher cropping ability, in addition to the season of maturity. Some of the varieties were raised in America, chiefly those that ripen very early, but for sheer quality, the late British ones are most often far superior. You must decide which you want.

Peaches: Varieties

There are indications that the varieties, like almost everything else, are being streamlined, it being uneconomical for nurserymen to propagate those for which there is little demand. I have checked through several catalogues and included here most of those names that appear in them, either consistently, or infrequently. In one or two instances the descriptions are those given by the nurseries, but more often they are my own observations through having cultivated them in gardens where I have worked.

'Amsden's June.' A popular peach on account of earliness. It came from America nearly 100 years ago. Ripens in early July. Fruits are medium size, greenish-white, flushed red, while flesh is rather soft and sweet.

'Barrington.' A large, yellow-skinned peach, striped or mottled crimson. It has pale flesh, red at the stone, and ripens in mid-September. It has a most delicious flavour, and is easy to grow. Has been in existence for a century and a half. I am fond of this peach.

'Bellegarde.' Arrives about the same time as 'Barrington'. It is large and completely covered with deep crimson. The flesh is yellow, red at the stone, and possesses a very good flavour. It is much loved by exhibitors, as well as connoisseurs.

'Crimson Galande.' The largish fruit ripens during August, and is liked by some gardeners because it is ready for flower shows, the colour being deep crimson. The flesh is soft and red at the stone. Not a really good flavour unless gathered at the right moment.

'Duke of York.' An early July peach with brilliant crimson fruits that are melting and refreshing. Quite a useful variety if flavour is not a criterion.

'Dymond.' This matures early September. It has a greenish tinge to the yellow skin that is shaded dull red. Flesh is white, red at the stone, and melting. Flavour is remarkably good. Tree grows well. I like this variety very much.

'Hale's Early.' A variety that is planted very frequently. It ripens in July, and is a typical American introduction. Flesh is white and melting, but the size is disappointing. Although quite hardy, I do not recommend it.

'Lady Palmerston.' Late September. A beautiful and very rich variety with dark orange-yellow flesh, being a seedling of the nectarine, 'Pine Apple'. Needs warmth, but a very choice peach to grow.

'Peregrine.' I have grown this variety more often than any other, regarding it as the best one ripening in August. It is probably the most valuable of the many peaches raised by Rivers. The handsome fruits are brilliant crimson and have a lovely appearance. The pale flesh is nicely firm and juicy. While it has not the flavour of some later varieties, it is ideal in all other respects.

'Prince of Wales.' A Michaelmas fruit with pale skin mottled red.

The flesh tastes and resembles a nectarine, it originating from one named 'Pitmaston Orange'.

'Rochester.' A yellow-fleshed peach much praised for outdoor cultivation. The season is mid-August and size is medium to large. It has a yellowish skin, flushed deep crimson, and ripens much the same time as 'Peregrine'. For indoors, it is not as desirable, or as easy to grow as the favourite.

'Royal George.' A pale-skinned peach with blood-red cheek, that ripens in early September. The flesh is pale yellow, with red near the stone. It is sweet and richly flavoured. A wonderful peach where a little heat is given.

'Sea Eagle.' A very late, large peach of pale lemon colour with dark crimson flush. The flesh is pale deepening near the stone. The flavour is first-class. I have found it excellent when treated well.

'Violette Hâtive.' Mid-September. A large pale yellow fruit with dark red flush. Flesh is tender and juicy and of excellent flavour. Has stood the test of 300 years' cultivation.

'Waterloo.' An American variety of medium size that ripens in July. It has a green skin with red cheek and mottlings. There are other peaches better than this one. It is probably one of the earliest to ripen and explains why it is grown.

Nectarines: Varieties

Generally, the nectarines are somewhat more tender than peaches, although nectarines originate from peaches or vice versa. Being less likely to succeed outdoors, or even on walls, there is a more conservative list of varieties. Here are a few most frequently listed.

'Dryden.' Very large for a nectarine. Deep purple-red skin, with white flesh. Flavour is excellent but less sweet than some. Mid-August nectarine of good quality.

'Early Rivers.' End of July. A large fruit, light yellow, with brilliant crimson shading. Flesh greenish-white, of rich flavour. First-class for an early variety.

'Elruge.' Late August. Medium size. Pale greenish skin with very dark red flush. Flesh white and of excellent flavour. Has been in cultivation for 300 years. One of the hardiest varieties.

'Humboldt.' Mid-August. Large bright yellow skin with dark

crimson mottlings. Flesh is orange-coloured and juicy. It is a free-bearer, and most satisfying.

'John Rivers.' A valuable nectarine ripening in mid-July. The fruits are golden and covered with dark crimson stripes. Flavour is first-class. A nice choice for an unheated house, where earliness is desirable.

'Lord Napier.' This is a large, pale yellow variety well covered with dark crimson, and ripens in early August. The white flesh is refreshing and of rich flavour. The skin is somewhat thin and is easily damaged, otherwise this is a good nectarine.

'Pine Apple.' A deep orange and rich crimson handsome fruit ripening in early September. The yellow flesh is most delicious and well flavoured. It is the best of all nectarines in, or out, of its season. Mr. Rivers raised it from the 'Pitmaston Orange' variety.

'Pitmaston Orange.' As above, but has a darker skin and a more sugary flavoured flesh.

'Spenser.' A little later than the last two, covered in crimson, being very dark on the sunny side. The flesh is reddish throughout and has rich flavour. A favourite exhibition fruit.

'Violette Hâtive.' Like the peach of the same name, it is a very old variety. Has wonderful flavour and ripens early.

When choosing varieties of peaches or nectarines some account should be taken of the position and locality. It may pay, in spite of the variety being of mediocre quality, to have one that is early, rather than one that is late. Late varieties are only superior when they have adequate warmth right through the ripening stages. Therefore, unless the locality is a warm one and the greenhouse is in a sunny position, the late varieties should be looked at askance.

Under good normal conditions where a modicum of warmth is provided when necessary and there is sufficient room in a greenhouse to accommodate two trees—the peach 'Peregrine' and the nectarine, 'Pine Apple', make an ideal pair.

9—Planting and Training

The house having been fitted with the wire trellis, and the borders prepared, the trees should be planted directly they arrive from the nursery, at any time during late autumn or winter. Upon arrival they are unpacked, examined, and damaged roots or branches trimmed back to healthy wood. The roots are then stood in a bucket, or tub, of water for about two hours. But if it is impossible to plant them immediately, they are unpacked and the roots temporarily buried (laid in), in damp soil, preferably outdoors. In this case the roots are then immersed in water for about an hour just before planting.

The hole for the first tree is dug out of the prepared border, under the trellis so that the tree will, when held in position, have the fan-trained branches slightly forward and in alignment with the wire trellis. The tree itself will tell you which side to put towards the front. The roots will probably be lop-sided, as will the branches incline forwards or backwards. They should incline towards the interior of the house. The depth of planting must be the same as when growing in the nursery, or slightly deeper. This is apparent by the change of colour of the bark a few inches above the roots. Never adjust the depth to fit the wire trellis. If the lowest horizontal branches are not in alignment with the bottom wire, adjustments must be made when training the trees later.

Having determined the depth, and spread the roots in the dug hole naturally, one starts to cover them. But before doing so, I personally like to get some fine damp sedge peat, and mix it into the excavated soil to make it more pliable. It will then, when thrown over the roots, trickle down among them nicely. The tree should also be jogged up and down gently to help this. When necessary, some is pressed down into the crevices with the fingers. Once the root bunch is hidden, more soil is piled on top and then pressed down firmly with the feet so complete the job properly. But if the soil is rather dry, when the roots have been covered, and before the top is added, a good soaking is given them, with tepid water from a fine-rosed can. They are then left to drain a few hours before the topsoil is added and firmed down. The flopping branches are now loosely attached to the wires, but not secured.

Once the trees have settled and the surface is dryish, they are ready to be given the most drastic pruning. It could be done before planting, but I prefer to keep the young whippy branches on the trees at that stage, in order to give guidance in exact positioning.

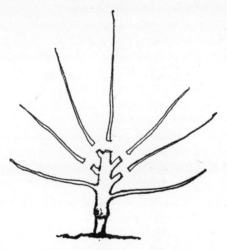

FIG. 14. Method of pruning, fairly drastically,
a newly planted tree the first time

First Pruning

The primary object of the first pruning is to cut the tree back so hard that it will produce new shoots in such a way that the shape will be truly like a fan. If this is not done the tree will have a strong middle and next to no sides. There are too frequent examples of this where the planters have been afraid to prune so drastically, or are greedy and want fruit before the tree is strong enough to bear it.

As explained in the last chapter, good two-year-old trees have five, seven, or more branches, with the middle one directly above the main stem. This one is cut out, right down to where the next

5. This peach tree shows points of cultivation described in the text; the stem below the graft union is slightly smaller than it is above it, and the main branches are splayed with no upright ones (some foliage has been removed to show the fruit).

6. A fig trained against a wall showing the first crop of the season.

branch veers to right or left, using a sharp knife and paring the wound. This is to ensure that goodness goes into the side branches more equally, instead of this one taking more than its share, as it surely would if left (see Fig. 14).

Next, pay attention to the lowest branches growing on either side, merely snipping off the tips and tying them to the lowest wire. They will rarely be flush with the wire or straight enough to be fixed neatly. However, they can generally be gently pulled to the, more or less, horizontal position. But, at this stage they should not be bent down lower than the point at which they emanate from the main stem. If it is necessary, fix them instead to the second wire up.

The ends should be snipped off so that there is always a single wood-bud left at the extremities.

Wood-buds

There are on peach trees, as with most tree fruits, two distinguishable sorts of buds—those that produce new shoots and those that produce flowers. Sometimes they are separate, and sometimes they are in bunches. On young trees the wood-buds dominate, while on some of the older trees there are too many flower-buds. They are easily discernible, and should always be recognised by the grower.

Wood-buds are narrow and long, and cling more closely to the stems than do flower-buds.

The flower-buds are more stubby, rounded, and stand out well. Sometimes the flower-buds are referred to as fruit-buds, although they may not always be that. Invariably they yield flowers of sorts, but not necessarily fruits.

When pruning, the cut should be made just above a single wood-bud, so that the tree can grow from the extremity, which it cannot do if there is only a flower-bud.

A compacted bunch of buds will often be found at the end of the unpruned shoots, which will, when the growing season comes, start to extend the tree area. However, if you cut back to a good wood-bud, this bud will produce a growing shoot that will be more vigorous than the one remaining if the end is not removed. Therefore, to encourage that lowest pair of horizontal branches to grow outwards, we merely shorten them in the dormant season. Having shortened the lower branches slightly and

G   97

completely removed the middle one we now have left two or three unpruned oblique branches on each side. These we shorten to within a few inches of the main stem, doing so just above healthy wood-buds. The ones most upright are cut back harder than those lower down. But at no time is there a regularised measurement of cutting. Most often, the stronger ones are not pruned as severely as the thinner ones. Nevertheless, they are shortened considerably, for the whole object is to get plenty of strength into the lower part of the tree framework, and this method of pruning will cause new strong shoots to sprout from the wood-buds that are left.

All trees have a tendency to put most of their energy into the buds at the ends of branches and shoots, rather than into the base. This kind of pruning regulates the tendency.

With the seasonal treatment, watering, spraying and ventilating, as indicated in the next chapter the hard-pruned young tree will soon produce strong young shoots from practically all wood-buds. If all were allowed to grow, there would soon be a thicket. Then it would necessitate extensive pruning in winter. But we avoid that by disbudding those that will not be wanted.

Disbudding

Remembering that, at this stage, we are more concerned with the filling out of the branches, rather than the bearing of fruits, we encourage all those new shoots that we think will make excellent branches within the main framework. Obviously, the shoots at the ends growing from the extreme wood-buds are needed. There may be a few others growing on the same shortened branches, equally desirable, to form sub-branches. But it is unlikely that any shoots growing to the front or any that grow backwards towards the glass are wanted, therefore these can be disbudded.

In this connection, to disbud simply means picking a young shoot off the branch with the fingers. I should explain that there are other instances in the cultivation of flowers when disbudding means the removal of flower-buds. We never disbud the flowers on peach trees. We thin the fruits instead. But we do disbud the young shoots coming from wood-buds, when they are unwanted.

Having disbudded the unwanted shoots, and so encouraged the others to grow, the latter must be tied loosely into position with raffia, either to the stems of the branches, or to the wires, or to pieces of cane fixed to the wires vertically.

The Second Winter

In the first dormant season, a year after planting, we start a routine pruning and cleaning by first releasing the branches from the wires, and either sponging them with an insecticide, or spraying with tar oil. Modern growers spray. Old ones sponge, taking care to do this from the middle of the tree towards the ends of the branches and shoots, so as not to damage the buds. That done, each branch and its shoots are put back against the wires and tied in strategic places, with soft fillis twine. It is usual to start with the lowest horizontal branches on either side.

The year previously, just after planting, we only pruned the lowest branches by snipping off the ends. They will, or should, have now, in addition to a strongish new extension of growth from the end bud, several shoots growing along the branches from the wood-buds. If the branches have been given the dis-budding treatment as suggested in a previous paragraph, they will now have several shoots that are growing upwards or downwards, but not any projecting forwards, or growing towards the glass.

These shoots that are left will have upon them, most probably, some single wood-buds, some flower-buds, either singly or in pairs, and sometimes with two flower-buds, and a wood-bud in between them, forming 'triple buds'.

Most often, the wood-buds are at the base of the shoots, and at the growing end, while the flower-buds are in the middle part. To know this will help the grower to control all the pruning and disbudding of peach and nectarine trees. If he understands that he will know just what to do.

During the summer to come, it will be perfectly all right to allow one or two fruits to develop from the flowers on the best of the side-shoots of the lowest pair of branches, but it will be detrimental to allow more. We are still much more concerned with the future welfare of the tree than getting instant results.

Shoots that Bear Fruit

Throughout, I have purposely refrained from using technical jargon, such as 'laterals' and 'sub-laterals' (as for vines), as these can become confusing, and instead I have used the words 'branches' and 'shoots'. For me the branches are the main parts

99

that form, as it were, the ribs of the fan. Obviously, if they were simple and singular, there would be great gaps around the outer part of the fan, while the middle would be crowded. Therefore, in due course, the mature tree has a framework of 'sub-branches', due to the deltoid divisions we cause by pruning the branches where appropriate.

It is on the shoots that grow from the branches and sub-branches that we get flowers and fruit. Having grown during one spring and summer, and then fruited the next, they become a superfluous hindrance rather than a help, on a trained tree, but if

Fig. 15. Method of pruning a one-year-old shoot that has produced fruit and also some new shoots from the base that are now retained

we completely removed them, it is obvious that there would be nothing left but the ribs (branches), and any fresh shoots that grew in consequence would not bear fruit in that same year. We are saved by the fact that the wood-buds at the basal end of the year-old shoots will produce other shoots, near the branches, or sub-branches. Thus, when winter comes and we prune and overhaul the trees we, at the same time, cut off the shoots that have borne fruits back to the point where new shoots have formed, so that these new shoots replace the old ones in the network (see Fig. 15).

However, it stands to reason that all the shoots of the previous year have not been allowed to bear fruit, simply because we have thinned the crop most severely. But we treat these as though they had, i.e. they are cut off just above new shoots growing from the base.

I have so far deliberately over-simplified the procedure. Each tree is an individual, and there are no clear-cut good rules upon pruning or disbudding. I have striven to impart the principles so that the new grower can possibly grasp them, and apply them to the trees under cultivation. Provided that you know what you are doing you can do almost anything—but if one gets into a state of indecision, it becomes difficult. There are experienced growers who take great pains to describe the various forms of growths upon trees. If we can sense the tree's reaction to our curbings, that is a better guide.

To give one example, there are some trees that will sometimes send out the odd freak strong shoots from the lower parts, above the bud union, that are sappy, soft, and are sparsely budded. If the existing framework is healthy and has sufficient sub-branches and shoots, I would cut this freak shoot cleanly away. But, if the framework was weak and there were gaps, I would not hesitate to try to tame this shoot by tying it to the wires and training it in a downward curve, to try to make it less vigorous. In one instance I actually curved the branch round into a complete circle and then let the end grow up, to produce nice fruits.

When training fans it is also helpful to realise that when a branch is bent downwards it will grow less vigorously than when allowed to grow upwards. Therefore, if the tree is lopsided, the branches on the heavy side should be pulled down as much as is practically possible, while the other side is allowed to develop. Sometimes it even pays to take a branch right across from one side to the other. There are no rules. But there must be understanding.

Quite often, branches will become bare at the base, leaving a hard, wooden framework with no lower shoots. In that case, it is well to try and obtain a new leader from one at the base, if possible, so that when this grows, the old piece can be cut away immediately above it. But if that is impossible, i.e. an old branch does not send forth new growth from the base, it is quite likely that another will have a strong shoot that can be trained across the pattern, so that it entirely and completely replaces the old branch, which is amputated at its base.

I could be criticised for not giving more details about stopping shoots, i.e. nipping off the ends when they have grown beyond their allotted space. It can, and is done, but I think it more imperative to know how the tree behaves than to dwell on technicalities. I personally have hardly ever 'stopped' a shoot, whether or not it has been allowed to produce fruit. It is tied in, just to keep the shape tidy, or completely removed, preferably by disbudding. But always, it is borne in mind that the new shoot, to replace it in the next season, comes from its base, as already described. Once you understand the sense of it, it becomes quite straightforward. But if you worry over a maze of instructions you will more likely go wrong.

10–The Year's Routine

We now go on to see what treatment is necessary during the year, once trees reach the bearing stage. It is best, I think, to go through the four seasons, rather than attempt anything like a monthly calendar. This can be applied to all trees, whether forced, or whether the reader lives in a warm or a cold climate.

Winter Treatment

The period between November and approximately mid-February is when we give the trees as much ventilation as possible, whether or not there is artificial heat. And regardless of the weather.

As soon as possible after the foliage falls in late autumn, but not before, the whole of the branches are released from the wire trellis, pruned where necessary, and then cleaned with an insecticide. A very weak (5 per cent) solution of tar oil wash can be used, provided that the buds have not swollen.

After the pruning has been done, and the woodwork and glass cleaned, the branches and shoots are tied back to the wires and then the roots in the border are given a thorough soaking. They are now left to rest until the buds begin to swell.

Spring Treatment

When the buds show signs of swelling, the ventilators are closed at night, but are opened during the day whenever the temperature is mild. The trees are syringed with clear water each morning when the air is warm. This is repeated again in the afternoon on mild, dryish days. To some extent, as with vines, you let your own feelings regulate your treatment for the trees. If it feels warm in a sheltered place, but there is a chill wind blowing, you merely put on a crack of air by opening the top ventilator a little way. But if the air is muggy and the wind feels balmy, there is no harm in giving as much ventilation as possible, even leaving the door open.

As emphasised in Chapter 7, the borders have to be well drained but they should never be allowed to become dry. One must watch, especially when damping down or using mist sprays that make the surface damp, that the soil below is not dry. It is useless to give dribs and drabs. One good watering, ensuring that it goes right through the border of about 2 gallons per square yard on an average soil, should last two months in winter, about three weeks in early spring, and a fortnight in summer. One can check by pushing a stick into the soil or by watching the trees. If the leaves droop, for instance, or there is a feeling of dryness, a thorough soaking is probably essential.

Pollination

The flowers, when they open, generally come out in very large numbers and make a lovely display. If the ventilators are open the bees will enter and do some of the pollination. This is seldom enough, therefore we brush the face of the flowers, so taking pollen from one to another. The traditional puff was a rabbit's tail on a stick. If difficult to find, a smooth-haired brush, such as those used for cleaning camera and projector lenses, will be just as good. It will be helpful to spray the flowers gently, with an atomiser. Never be forceful at this stage.

Immediately the flower petals die, syringe more forcefully once again. And when the days are warm one should also sprinkle water upon the footways and walls during midday. The ventilators are closed by night, especially when the weather is cold, but opened by day.

With the fruitlets come new green shoots that sprout from the wood-buds. These, like the fruitlets, will be far more numerous than the number wanted. We must remember that they will bear next year's crop, just as the present one is mostly found on last year's growths. Now, we more or less see plainly where we want next year's shoots to grow and where not to grow. Those we want, either for bearing fruit or sometimes for filling gaps in the tree structure, are retained, while those obviously unwanted are rubbed off. This rubbing off, or disbudding, is not done hurriedly, but piecemeal. Any that grow too near clefts, or point towards the glass, or grow boldly into the house, are undesirable. One tries to produce herring-bone effect, with the main ribs forming a pattern as in the veins of leaves.

Fruit Thinning

It is at this time that thinning the fruitlets is begun. I like to start when they are the size of hazel nuts. Other people prefer to begin earlier. But they are not all thinned at once. Just like the shoots, the positions of the fruitlets are considered. At this stage it is mostly a matter of reducing the number of overcrowded ones (see Fig. 16).

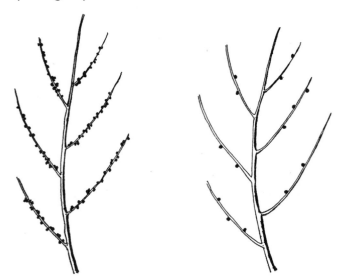

FIG. 16. An overcrowded branch of fruitlets, left, and the same branch after thinning. This is not the complete and final thinning stage

Summer Treatment

Assuming the summer period to be from about the middle of May until late August, the new shoots and the young peach fruits can be seen growing fairly rapidly. The chief jobs are spraying morning and evening, and damping down during the day. This can be eased by modern equipment. Automatic mistifiers can be employed, and also indoor irrigation units.

The worst indoor pest is red spider mite. This comes when the air is too dry, and the temperature is too warm. Constant syringeing is the best means of keeping it away.

Ventilation is imperative. Although there are thermostat ventilator controls available, they are not as good as personal attention. Notwithstanding, they can be useful if you are not an early riser. The ventilators should be opened very early in the mornings, before the sun shines too strongly, or the foliage becomes scorched. Another way, in the summer, is to leave a little air on all and every night.

Continue to disbud the shoots and also to thin the fruitlets. The new shoots will become more prominent and it is possible to see where any need to be removed, or should be retained. Generally, the desired shoots are those that sprout from the base of the existing ones below where the fruits are borne. If there are gaps in the general pattern of the fan-shaped trees, some shoots are retained and encouraged to grow, so that they will ultimately fill the spaces. But for the moment, they are loosely tied back until the winter.

It is now when the first fertiliser is given. It should be a good standard formula containing a predominance of potash, but should also have all the other elements. It is scattered over the border inside the house at the rate recommended by the makers, lightly prodded into the surface, and then watered in. Most gardeners favour branded dressings, such as Bentley's Peach and Nectarine Fertiliser. I have before now used a proprietary tomato food because it contained a good quantity of potash.

Stoning Period

About late May, or early June, the fruitlets left upon the shoots will seem to stop growing. They are forming stones. After a while they will begin to swell again, and, if any further thinning is done, as it should be, you will, if one or two are cut through, find the hard centre, which shows that all is well. At this stage the final thinning should be carried out, leaving only about a dozen peaches over each square yard of the fan area, but if dealing with nectarines, one can leave a score. It is a matter of judgement which to leave. Those of good size that have unimpeded room to swell are favoured, while those in awkward places or at the tips of weak shoots are picked off.

Once the fruits begin to grow well, a second application of fertiliser is given at the same rate as before, i.e. 3 oz. per square yard of border if Bentley's Peach Fertiliser was used. Always see that the roots never lack water, and that spraying is regular.

Borders and walls are damped down each midday, and ventilators are kept open day and night.

Autumn Treatment

Assuming that the last quarter of our calendar starts when the fruit ripens, which can be any time from very late July until October, according to variety, spraying is done regularly until there are apparent signs of ripeness; this is then stopped until the crop is gathered.

Water should not be applied to the border while the fruit is actually ripening.

Once the peaches have attained full size, any leaves that stop the light and sunshine from beaming on them should be picked off, or tied aside. The fruit does not have stalks, but is attached to the shoots so closely that the back flesh is grooved by them, and if you tug too strongly there is bruising. The careful gardener only tries to gather when the individual peaches are considered to be almost ready to fall off. He pushes his fingers along behind the fruit parallel with the shoot, so that it is between the third and fourth fingers, and then he very gently, but firmly, pulls it away. The gathered fruit is then placed in a cool room, preferably on clean paper, until needed.

It is usual, and wisely so, to put a catch net or straw-bed under the tree, in case fruit falls before gathering. Actually, it is reckoned that those that fall off are less flavoured than the ones picked just before this is likely. They have passed their peak.

All the ventilation possible should be given at the ripening stage. When kept too close the flavour is impaired. But that is no argument for preferring outdoor crops to those grown indoors. One almost always has so many losses and spoiled fruits when grown outside, and those 'harvested' have almost always been gathered long before they are ready. You can and do give your indoor fruit subtle treatment and attentions that are impracticable in the open.

Once all are harvested, as much air as is possible is allowed. The roots are heavily watered, and the tops syringed vigorously.

The leaves will eventually turn colour, and are often helped in the 'fall', by swishing them over with a besom broom, the idea being to expose the branches and shoots as much as possible before the sun loses its power.

Heated Houses

The only difference between the cultural treatments of unheated and heated houses is that growth stimulated by artificial heat means earlier starting.

In the spring, because heat causes early swelling of the buds, the ventilators must be controlled more carefully, and spraying started as early as is appropriate to the amount of heat given.

Early fruit is not as well flavoured as normal crops, and much care has to be taken to see that they get the maximum ventilation during the ripening stages.

It is bad to try to force trees one year and not the next. If forced one season they will be precocious the next. In large gardens there is often an 'early house', a 'cool house' and a 'late case', the latter being glass sashes sharply angled against a tall, warm wall with no heat other than that of the sun. But in all instances the general treatment is similar, only differing in the time of year. Generally, early varieties are forced, while the late ones are grown in unheated cases to provide fruit during late autumn.

Other Plants

The ideal policy is to make peacheries exclusive to peaches and nectarines. But that is hardly ever done. Late chrysanthemums are most often housed in them. As these demand just as much air as peaches no harm is done, provided that the pots are stood upon planks laid over the soil. Once the flowers have been gathered the old stools are removed to cold frames, or placed in the gangways of the houses.

Only those other flowers that do not interfere with the needs of the peaches and nectarines should ever be allowed in the greenhouse. That is a counsel of perfection, seldom carried out, but it is most advisable.

11–Peach Afflictions

Peaches and nectarines are subjected to physiological and parasitical afflictions just like most other vegetation. The outdoor trees become infected with the fungal peach leaf curl, which I have never yet seen in a greenhouse. The outdoor cultivator has to regularly spray with Burgundy, or Bordeaux Mixture to prevent this malady infecting the trees, and even when this is done it is not always entirely controlled.

There are a few fungal troubles that occur indoors, but nothing as serious as that. Perhaps the shot-hole disease is the most common. Small brown spots appear on the leaves that eventually expand and kill the tissue, leaving small holes that inspire the name. If it happens, the usual procedure is to spray with Burgundy or Bordeaux Mixture. Both these are based upon copper sulphate, the difference being that this acid is neutralised by the addition of lime in the Bordeaux formula, while for Burgundy it is washing soda. Either can be bought ready-mixed, and either will do.

Another possible, but hardly probable, bother is galls on the stems around the base at about soil level. They come from wounds, or over-wetness. Wounds should be dressed with white lead paint, while wetness of the soil should be rectified.

Powdery mildew is much commoner. It appears on the trees when there is too much or too little water at the roots, or where the interior temperatures fluctuate too much, or there are draughts. If the ventilators are opened so that there is not too much draught, and the trees syringed rather forcefully a few times, it will be washed off.

Remedial sprays are dinocap (or Karathane), provided the fruits are not fully developed, or green sulphur dusted about after spraying. But never mix such chemicals unless it is stated by manufacturers that they can be mixed. Chemical reactions can be disastrous.

Pests

Red Spider Mite

As with vines one of the worst bothers is red spider mite. This makes the leaves look extremely dirty and can spoil a good crop. Water syringed forcefully will harass them to death. If applied during the whole of the growing period prior to the ripening of fruit, the pest will be unlikely to spread so quickly during that brief period.

However, once it gets hold it becomes alarming. Although I never have hesitated to use azobenzene as an aerosol, or fumigant, on vines, I have never risked it on peaches. If there are any signs of red spider on the trees at ripening time, a spray of wettable derris is used. I never regard this as exceptionally potent, but it does check the bother.

Mealy Bug and Scale Insects

Mealy bug can be just as much a problem with peaches as with vines (which see), but I have found that scale insects have been more persistent. The most prominent of these is brown-coloured and shaped like a diminutive tortoise. It adheres to the stems like a limpet. A mild (5 per cent) diluted spray with tar oil in the dormant season is a good preventative. Should the insect be noticeable while leaves and fruit abound, a malathion aerosol or an ordinary spray will most times clear the trouble.

Malathion is a good insecticide for destroying red spider, white fly, aphids and thrips, as well as mealy bug and scale.

Aphids

Aphids, too, are controlled by the winter spray of tar oil, which kills the overwintering eggs. If there are outbreaks in summer, when they breed and spread with amazing rapidity, whether of the black, green or blue types, a spray with derris, or malathion, or a malathion smoke will clear them.

Their presence is evident when the new growing shoots have curly and twisted leaves. Another sign of their presence is ants that may be found crawling up and down the tree stems, feeding upon the juices the aphids yield when prodded by their proprietors.

The best way to deal with ants is to put down baits in their tracks, such as the proprietary Tugon or Nippon.

Woodlice

Woodlice are another nuisance, spoiling the fruits close to where they are attached to the shoots. I have known experienced gardeners to become frantic about them, and to have adopted all sorts of antidotes, such as putting swabs of cotton wool soaked in methylated spirit as closely as they dare to the ripening fruits.

Woodlice spend their days in wall crevices, under wooden duckboards, or in mulching litter; another place they like to hide, if they can, is in the bottom of pots among the drainage crocks. If it is made impossible for them to breed or hide, much of the bother is stopped. But when that cannot be done, 'Sevin Dust', sprinkled around where they are likely to be, will stop them.

There are one or two other pests of the insect world that occasionally enter the peach house, but, if routine sprayings or smokes are carried out against any of those pests just mentioned, no others will be likely to survive.

Functional Disorders

Split Stones

I have never found this irritating bother very worrying among indoor peaches, but have at times experienced it on outdoor wall crops. When the fruit separates from the tree stem, there is a hole in the cavity, and the stone is hollow, while the flesh is of inferior quality.

The split stone complex in a tree has been said to be due to many things. Lack of lime is one, yet we are assured by experts that it is not so. Fluctuations in temperatures and watering may cause it. Another possibility is imperfect pollination. If any of these shortcomings can be rectified so much the better. I have found early varieties more susceptible than those that ripen later.

Another occasional upset results in the leaves being pale and anaemic-looking. When trees are like that they are unhealthy. Some regard this as a shortage of iron. Others attribute it to an excess of lime, which in itself leads to a deficiency of iron within the tree. This could well be. A dressing of proprietary sequestrene will do no harm, in fact may bring about the desired good health, and also rectify split-stone.

Bud Dropping

Whereas I have never found this trouble on outdoor peaches, indoor trees will sometimes shed their buds in early spring, leaving long bare gaps up the shoots. I am confident that this is due to allowing the roots to become dry during winter. When flowers are brought in, with the pots being placed on the borders, the surface may appear to be moist, while the roots below are suffering from extra dryness.

One of my fetishes has been always to give the indoor peach roots a thorough soaking in December. In one instance I made a lad soak the border three times because I was not satisfied that he had done it thoroughly enough at the first and second attempts. No buds dropped that spring. After all, it is natural for outdoor trees to have their roots thoroughly soaked while they are resting.

Chemicals

I can think of no more problems. But one may be in the inexperienced or sentimental grower being concerned about the use of pesticides that may be dangerous to birds, animals, or human beings. There are some very dangerous chemicals in existence. On the other hand, some are less dangerous than the old poisons that gardeners used. Before I apply any chemical I study Ministry of .Agriculture Lists and heed all the cautionary notes on the container. If they are too extensive I never use that one.

And any that are used are diluted strictly to the strength advised, or, in most cases, much weaker. Tar oil can spoil buds as well as aphid eggs if used at the wrong season. Nothing is safe. But there is a likelihood of no harm being done if the least dangerous antidotes are used properly.

7. A crop of sweet melons just beginning to 'net', some of which already require supporting. Orchids are being grown beneath them.

12—Indoor Figs

We can best grow figs indoors by knowing a few facts about them, although some of these may seem to be irrelevant. They are quite different to any other form of vegetation except to members of their own order. And even then they are so distinct from mulberries, for example, to which they are surprisingly related.

They are very ancient, of course, being mentioned in dramatic fashion both in the Old and New Testaments. These tell us that they abounded in the Middle East, which gives a clue to their needs in the way of sunshine.

We also know that the figs grown in British gardens are quite different, at least in appearance, to those that are filled with many seeds. The difference is that imported figs have been pollinated whereas ours are not. They are unlikely ever to be pollinated in this country, although I believe that there is a hormone spray being invented for that purpose.

The original story is that in their native country there are two sorts of figs, one being inedible, but grown to produce what are called 'caprifigs' inside which fig-wasps and pollen are produced. The wasps leave their incubator caprifigs and fly to the real figs, creeping into the interior with pollen upon them, so that fertilisation takes place. Consequently, in fig orchards there have to be mainly trees of edible figs interspersed with caprifigs, just as in the same way we have our apple variety pollinators.

As everyone should know, all the flowers of the fig are inside the fruit. The wasps that fertilise them do not live in Britain, hence our seedless crops. In consequence we get sweeter, more juicier and more desirable dessert fruits for those who like them.

One rich connoisseur, to my knowledge, loved the seedless figs his gardener grew so much that, if he were away from home, some were sent by air to wherever he happened to be. We were amused when the address was in Turkey.

The next fact to know about them is that they bear two or three

H   113

crops each year, but only one seems to mature, when grown outdoors, and even that one seldom yields to any extent. This is due
to several reasons, a lesser one being the bad treatment they get,
but which we can put right when we grow them indoors.

If you look at an outdoor fig tree in autumn, you will find many
half-developed fruits which will never come to any good. At the
ends of the new growths, beyond these, can be seen along the
tips some semblances of more figs threatening to grow. When the
leaves fall, the older half-grown figs will wither and drop, if not
picked off (which they should be), while those tiny embryos at
the extremities will remain semi-dormant until the spring. Then
they will grow into the first crop—if they survive the winter.

Then, when the new shoots grow in spring, other figlets form
in the axils of the leaves. These generally become abortive. But
if the summer is exceptionally warm, they, too, may develop into
edible figs. Furthermore, fresh growths will produce more embryo figlets, thus forming the embryos of a third crop. So,
whether there are two or three crops depends upon the varieties,
and the weather, and the geographical position. There is mostly
only one modest crop in our climate.

With that basic knowledge, we can study the conditions, and
the indoor treatment, to bring two or even three crops to fruition
each year.

Roots

The roots must be confined. If the tree is to be a largish one on a
sunny wall within the house, the bed should be of concrete, or
bricks, with a bottom that is drained when rubble is placed over
it, to a proper outlet. It need be no more than 30 in. deep. Over
the floor put a foot depth of brickbats, or old mortar rubble, or
loose chalk. And on that put a 3-in. layer of finer stuff. Fill up the
rest of the space with good loamy soil. If this is heavy add some
bonfire ashes (not coal). If it is light, mix a little powdered marl
into it. The border should be moisture retentive, yet excess
water must drain away. There should be no manure.

The width from back to front of the border need be no more
than 3 ft. It can be somewhat wider if the wall area is likewise
large. But always err on the side of confining the roots rather than
allowing them a free run.

If grown in pots, and this is quite a good method for indoor figs, the 9-in. size will do. Pots can be smaller or larger, the resulting trees being proportionate. Put crocks in the bottom for drainage, and for a potting mixture use crumbly loam, such as for chrysanthemums, but without the food. Instead, mix in plenty of old brick rubble.

Fig plants are mostly propagated from layers or cuttings, although they can also be raised from offsets, or by grafting. I think that cuttings make the best plants for indoor cultivation, especially in pots. But these can be difficult owing to the milky sap making rooting impossible. Layers are the easiest means of getting plants. These have simply been obtained by bending down branches to the ground and covering the place where each is pinned down with a small pile of soil. A cut should be made under the stem at the lowest point where it touches the ground, so stopping sap and causing roots to form. The best time is just as growths are starting in the spring, and layers should be ready for removal by the end of the year (see Fig. 17).

Fig. 17. Method of layering a fig branch.
Note the notch in the stem under the peg

Varieties

It is becoming more and more difficult to get a wide selection of varieties. Many fruit tree nurseries stock only 'Brown Turkey'. While it is one of the best figs, the more venturesome would like something different. One firm lists five others, three of which they recommend for greenhouse work.

One of these is 'Bourjassotte Grise', which is of medium size, rather flat and round, and is dark skinned with blood-red flesh that is more syrupy and juicy than most. Given pot cultivation it is a good bearer.

For a large expanse on a wall, 'Negro Largo' is a good choice. It is the largest fig that I know. The skin is black, and fruits are bulky and heavy, while the pale flesh is juicy and rich. We grew it outdoors in one garden and had some success with first crops only. It should do better indoors.

Although it is listed as an outdoor fig in the list of the same firm, 'White Marseilles' is quite a good variety for indoors, whether in a border or large pot, no matter whether the greenhouse is heated or not. It is very easy to grow.

I had several outdoor trees of 'White Marseilles' in one garden that actually bore a good second crop of nice fruits one glorious autumn following a good summer.

Indoor Methods

The normal time for outdoor figs to start forming new leaves is May. In a greenhouse that is kept ventilated and unheated except during frosty weather, the trees will start only a little earlier. Only in very good years, such as the one just mentioned, is one likely to have more than the first crop, the other aborting before the next ripening season.

But if the greenhouse is warmed earlier, say in February, so that plants can be raised from seed, or be grown on, the fig will also start to grow then, the resulting crop ripening in July, while the second one will be ready during September.

Three crops are most unlikely unless the grower takes much trouble and uses a lot of heat and guile in management. In that case, the leaves drop off in early October, and they are started into growth again in November. This is akin to battery chicken farming. The first crop comes in April, the second in June and July and the third in August and September.

Obviously, the best course is the middle one, i.e. an attempt to obtain two crops. The first will be a moderate one, while the second, if the trees are managed properly, will be a very successful one. In the open garden, as most people who have had fig trees know, this second crop that does not attain maturity is always considerably heavier than the first.

Water and Warmth

As with vines and peaches, figs will respond to warmth and moisture. The procedure is much the same in the early stages. When they are required to start into growth the ventilators are closed, and artificial warmth applied. The trees are syringed to try to create an atmosphere of buoyant humidity.

If there is no heat other than sunshine, less water is splashed around. Ventilators are opened when the sun is really warm, and closed early to shut the warmth in for the night.

But if an electric heater is available, with a fan, it can be set at 50° F. (10° C.) so that the night temperature does not fall dangerously low. And the ventilators can be kept more closed than for vines or peaches by day. They need not be opened before the temperature is 70° F. (21° C.) in the early stages, and later, it does no harm for the reading to be 90° F. (33° C.) before any air is given.

All the time the fruit and growths are forming, spraying is freely carried out. It stops red spider mite, helps growth, and aids the swelling fruitlets.

Topdressing

At this time the surface of the border, or the tops of the pots, are given a topdressing of rich compost. Old methods included mixing in fresh horse droppings, with some fine loam. Other ingredients have been bonemeal, together with charcoal and woodashes to aid health. A good mixture can be made by having 2 parts friable potting loam and 1 part very decayed manure, or garden compost, together with a little proprietary fertiliser such as is advocated for tomatoes or other fruits. A little lime rubble is also advantageous.

The topdressing is applied every year just when the leaves and first-crop fruitlets are starting to develop. The old dressing of the year before is cleared off immediately beforehand.

For pots, the usual procedure is to place a ring of turf, or fine mesh wire, in fact anything that will hold a 4-in. depth of topdressing above the pot rim. The difference between topdressing borders and pots is that the pots are dealt with twice yearly instead of once. After the first crop has been gathered, the new fruitlets will start to grow and another dressing is most helpful.

The old is removed from the top extension and also a few inches down into the pot, taking care for the second topdressing not to injure the roots too much.

Stimulants

During the periods when the fruits of the first and the second crops are actually swelling, they like a nitrogenous stimulant. This can be started a few weeks after the topdressing is done, and be given when the plants are healthily taking water, warmth, and given some ventilation when the thermometer soars.

A little nitrate of soda will help them along. Or nitro-chalk. I have been successful with saltpetre (potassium nitrate, nitrate of potash), a teaspoonful of which dissolved in a can of rain water, and sprinkled over the soil once a week, will help them grow well and keep them healthy. Such fertilisers should never be given when the border is dry, neither should any be allowed to spill on any greenery. Otherwise they are quite safe in small doses.

Watering

It cannot be reiterated too many times that watering is the main key of success. The roots should never be allowed to become really dry. In winter they will not need much. Then they should only be moist. When they start to grow in spring, the borders and pots must be watered more frequently, say every third or fourth day. By the time the hours of daylight are at their zenith and the sun is warm the border may need a daily drench, while the pots need attention twice each day.

Spraying should be in the early morning, damping down the pathways, etc., during midday, with another good spraying over during early evening, so that all loose water has dissipated by nightfall.

Ripening Periods

There must be quite a change of treatment when the first crop starts to colour, indicating that the ripening period is near. Spraying is stopped. The border and pots are kept as dry as possible without actually causing any damage to the trees through lack of moisture. One must remember that, while the first crop is ripening, the embryos of the next are still needing sustenance.

If you have an electric heater with a fan that works all the time regardless of heat, and the thermostat is set at 50° F. (10° C.), it will be just right. The air will be in constant motion while the nights will never become too cold.

During the ripening periods, of either the first, second, or third crops, they should be given no fertilisers, or excessive moisture. But the spraying should be continued right up to the time when the fruit is actually changing colour.

Gathering Figs

Once they begin to colour they should, if for home consumption, be allowed to stay on the trees until properly ripe. This is when the necks bend, so that the fruits droop and there are bursting seams in the skin upon the sunny side. There is generally a globule, or tear, in the eye of each one. Then lift and break them off carefully. They will come away more easily in the morning, rather than later in the day.

If they have to be despatched, they must be gathered just before they threaten to burst their seams. I have found that they pack as neatly as fancy chocolate, but instead of paper cups you envelop each one in a fig-leaf. I used to send many to market that way.

Winter Rest

Once the crop has been gathered, if there is a later one to come, the watering, spraying and feeding with topdressing, or stimulants, is resumed. But if there are no more crops to follow, it now becomes autumn, and the trees will tell you that they need the winter rest. The leaves turn colour, and eventually drop. Do not feed, but do still keep the borders watered. They will need far, far less; hardly any in the darkest weeks. Still, they should never become dry. We must remember that those embryos are at the extremities of the shoots, and need food until ready to grow when spring arrives.

Going back to the statement that some gardeners obtained three crops by allowing them only one month's rest, in October, this needs much skill and considerable heat. Trees are all the better if they get a natural winter, and are given at least two months' complete dormancy.

At the point when the leaves have all but fallen, root-pruning, by lifting and replanting, can be carried out.

Pruning

The training of the fig tree is somewhat difficult to describe because it can become involved. In the introductory remarks I stated a fact that is generally known about the fig bearing two or three crops, and that only the first one matures in this country, when grown in the open. In reality, very few outdoor figs produce a satisfactory crop of any kind. The embryos are killed by frost, or the trees, through lack of knowledge, are treated badly. Just because they need restricted root-runs, this infers they must be starved, yet they still have to be watered and fed at the right times.

Indoors, they will produce two crops quite well, and a third if they are supplied with lots of heat and food, and water in due season—and training. The growths have to be either pruned, pinched (stopped) or disbudded (rubbed).

We have ascertained that the trees are full of a milky substance that exudes at the slightest wounding. It soon heals upon growing shoots when young, but is more difficult when old stems are cut. Therefore, we can only prune when so doing is least likely to cause this excessive bleeding. Indoors, the best time is when the autumn leaves are falling. There are other beliefs that the best time is just as the plants are about to grow again in spring. Both are based upon experience.

We have ascertained that the figs produce their fruits at the extremities of the branches. Actually, they form embryo fruits at the tips continuously, as they grow, so that there is a steady formation of them, ready to grow when stimulated. However, they do do it in flushes, so that we more or less put them into first, second and third crops, each ripening in turn, while the successors 'follow on in front' at definite intervals.

At the end of the season, when winter comes, as it were, the figs that are unlikely to withstand the rigours of the weather are either shed by the tree or are killed by frosts and wet. However, those no larger than shirt buttons just forming along the extremities of the branches are akin to eggs that could stay dormant through the bad period, ready to develop when the time is opportune. These may develop with what we call the first crop. Those that follow them are waves of entirely new embryos on the new wood.

Therefore, we must have plenty of unpruned shoots, for if we prune them back the embryo fruits are removed. Yet, if you read books you will be told to pinch back at the fifth leaf, or the seventh leaf, or whatever, without any further explanation. Which, when I first read such advice, filled me with perplexity.

I also knew that all the growing shoots did not produce figlets, because they were weak and unable to do so. And if left entirely to their own devices, especially the strong growers, they became a barren thicket. The policy must be to control the growths of the tree so that each branch is strong, yet not sappy, and must have close-jointed branches, not too old, yet must not be pruned back hard, or the fruits would be removed.

Rubbing

The first control, then, is to rub off the tiny buds of prospective branches near the main stems of the tree. There must be enough left to grow so that new branches can form, either to replace the old worn-out ones or fill gaps in the general pattern, especially of a fan-trained tree. This rubbing off with the fingers of these tiny growths is done through the season in leisurely fashion, rather than in one foul attack.

In time, the old branches become far too long, and must be replaced by others, either sprouting from the stump of the tree or by sub-branches sprouting from the extenuated ones. When these are to take the places of the oldest, the latter must be pruned away cleanly, and if in the greenhouse they are best done at leaf-fall.

Pinching

The other treatment is stopping, or pinching. This is done when young trees are forming, at the expense of the current fruit, for future development. If the tree is to be a small standard in a pot, its topmost tip is pinched out, during the growing period, when it is about 2 ft. tall, nipping off the top few inches with finger-nails. Side-shoots follow. These are also nipped off when several inches long, the aim being to have a pyramidal-shaped tree. The new side-shoots from these should then bear fruit.

If allowed to grow willy-nilly, these sub-branches would soon attain unwieldy proportions. So, when fruit is forming that will eventually ripen, the new figs at the tip are pinched off to where the first crop (or second if indoors) is maturing. The outcome of that is that other sub-shoots will break from the stem further back. If they are overcrowded, some are rubbed off in the tiny stage. The others are allowed to form, and if it is some time before leaf-fall these will produce figlets the size of shirt buttons that will survive the winter and become the first crop of the next season.

In the case of young fan-trained trees, the growing shoots are nipped out to make side-branches form, and then by diligent stopping and some rubbing off of the tiny shoots, the whole space in time becomes covered with good branches.

There is considerable judgement needed. If you think that the latest fruitlets will get larger than peas, or shirt buttons, and are unlikely to survive the winter, the growing tips should be pinched back so that side-shoots can likely take their places.

Suckers

Fig trees often develop suckers at the base. These are either weak or too rank. They are seldom good fruiting stems, and should be removed while small. Fig trees should have single stems. Often these are not more than big stumps, with new branches growing up off them in spready fashion. This is good for fan-trained specimens.

I have noticed that many old trained trees have too much wood in them, often hefty stems sprouting just one or two feeble branches. In those circumstances, the thing to do is to encourage new branches to grow along the base, just above the top of the stump, and then take away one or two of the old stems each year in autumn. In this way, in time, there is rejuvenation.

If the fig grower is successful it may be that some crops will need thinning out, especially the credited second crop. The fruitlets about the size of walnuts should be reduced so that there are only three or four on each branch, those farthest from the growing tip being the ones to save.

And always, those figlets as large as marbles should all be picked off if they are hanging on when the leaves fall. They will never mature.

Fig Troubles

Generally, figs do not have troubles. They may have a touch of canker, of the sort that affects apples, in heated houses, but rarely attacks outdoor or coolly grown trees. If there is any it is cut off.

We had a disease in one garden on the outdoor trees which we called 'dirty nose'. Instead of the fruits ripening properly, the eye end of the fruit turned a pinkish colour and eventually became decayed. It was caused by a fungus, so I am told, and the only cure is to give them better drained and more airy conditions.

There is a physical defect at times which results in the young fruits being discarded when young, instead of beginning to swell. It is common with the variety 'Bourjassotte Grise' and there have been opinions that it is due to lack of fertilisation. There are now sprays being used to create fertilisation artificially. It is hardly feasible to me, for if you have fertilisation you surely must have seeds. We do not want seedy figs.

Incidentally, there is a school of thought, centuries old, that insist that if you put a drop of olive oil on the eye of each fig just as it is beginning to ripen it will do so more quickly and surely. There is no harm in trying this.

Pests

When grown badly, figs are prone to much the same pests as peaches and grapes, i.e. red spider mite, scale, mealy-bug. The same remedies apply.

It is inadvisable to use azobenzene on fig trees. Instead, a petroleum oil insecticide will control pests much more safely. One is sold under the trade name of Summer Stock Emulsion, packed by Plant Protection. It is for use under glass against red spider, mealy-bugs, scale insects and thrips. But, really, in the case of figs, prevention is better than cure.

I find it very difficult to prepare a calendar of operations for figs. Owing to the various ways of growing them a month-by-month guide would confuse, rather than be helpful. Feeding, watering, ventilating and training the branches are so inter-related, and necessary according to the varying stages of the crops that actual times cannot be given.

13—Trees in Pots

Growing fruit trees in pots or containers may be the only method in some greenhouses where it is impossible to fit proper wires and trellises. This is not really an economical way of growing fruit, but it is good fun. However, it stands to reason that watering has to be carried out more diligently, for pots do dry out quicker than beds. Yet, these being of considerable size are far less trouble than is the case with smaller plants that need this attention so frequently.

Having dealt with, in considerable detail, the cultivation of the three main crops—vines, peaches and nectarines—and figs, there is no more to do here than to consider those aspects so far ignored. How to grow figs in pots has been dealt with in the last chapter, for it is a very practical way of growing them.

Vines

I also referred to the growing of vines in pots. These are best grown on the long-rod system. This means having two forms of canes or stems on the same plant simultaneously. They are treated much as outdoor rambler roses. There is the cane that bears the current crop, and at the same time there is the new shoot that will bear the next crop. The older growth is cut away at the base each winter directly the leaves fall, so leaving only next year's cane, until new suckers grow from the base in due course.

There are four bamboos or sticks put down the inside of the large pot, so that they form a square, projecting upwards like an inverted pyramid. Around these the fruiting cane is wound two or three times in spiral fashion. It is generally kept about 4 ft. long, having been stopped in the previous year when at that length. The new one is allowed to grow up inside the other, and is lightly attached to the structure, and has its end nipped out when about 4 ft. in length, as just stated. All other growths, from the base, or the sides of the new growth, are pinched back after two leaves have formed.

The fruit will be produced on laterals on the one-year-old cane, just as on an established rod, and these are treated in precisely the same way as for the border vine. The pot-bound vines must be fed at much the same times as those growing in borders. In fact, give them the same treatment.

You can place pot vines outdoors in winter; in fact, it is better for them to be exposed than to be coddled in a greenhouse alone with other plants that need warmth.

But I would not stand figs outdoors. They are quite hardy, really, but do tend to be cut back by cold when too soft. If the greenhouse is too warm, they can be placed in a cool shed during the winter.

Other Fruits

I have grown quantities of gages and sweet cherries in pots. Apples and pears can also be grown that way. In the old days, it was one of the methods of obtaining specially refined crops for exhibition. At one time, a famous firm used to display collections of pot fruits at national shows. This is nothing new. Such efforts seem to have disappeared because of economic necessity. Nevertheless, I think this form of cultivation quite feasible, and suited to many small modern greenhouses in which it is impossible to grow flowers successfully.

I have not included apricots in this form of cultivation. They are very individualistic and very temperamental. I have tried to grow them several times but have never mastered the art. I do not recommend them for garden greenhouses.

Peaches and nectarines can also be grown in pots. But their system of fruiting on one-year-old shoots makes it rather difficult to restrict them to the usual pruning without knowing a good deal about how to train them so that they form fruiting spurs.

This goes for morello cherries too. They are spready subjects, and need plenty of space if they are to give good crops.

However, sweet cherries, gages, pears and apples will submit to having their shoots pinched back in summer. They are allowed to grow fairly long, and the tips are then nipped off, leaving only five leaves upon the shoot. This most frequently causes them to form fruiting spurs.

One of the first things to do is recognise which are fruiting buds and which are purely leaf buds. The leaf buds are long and thin and cling to the stem. The fruit buds are fat and round on the plum and peach fraternity, while for apples and pears they are stubby, much like chickens' toes or 'spurs'.

Trees should be specially chosen for this purpose, being propagated on dwarf rootstocks. If you tell the reliable nurserymen you need the most dwarf rootstocks, they will help you.

Practically all sweet cherries, many plums and gages, and some apples are self-sterile, and need compatible companions. This is another matter to discuss with the nursery.

However, if they are hand pollinated, by using the rabbit's tail, or brush, as mentioned in the chapters about peaches, it is found that the ones with bad reputations for pollination will fruit much better than they do outdoors.

The best time to start growing fruit in pots is early autumn. The bigger the pots the better. They should be generously crocked and roughage placed over this to stop the soil sinking down too quickly.

Compost

A good recipe for compost is 5 parts good fibrous loam; 1 part very decayed manure; 1 part old mortar rubble; $\frac{1}{2}$ part moist sedge peat, or good leafmould (all parts by bulk) and sharp sand according to texture. If this is heavy, a good deal should be added, but if on the light side add none at all. To each garden wheelbarrow-load mix in 2 5-in. potfuls of bonemeal, and 1 5-in. potful of a good general compound fertiliser, such as one sold specially for tomato cultivation.

After potting, stand the trees outdoors. Shortly after, the pots should be placed in a deep bed of ashes. If possible they should be covered to the pot rims, placing them fairly closely together. Later still, in the New Year, the whole surface is covered with litter to keep the roots warm, but the tops are left completely exposed.

In February, or just when they are showing signs of buds swelling, they are taken into the greenhouse; here they are kept as cool as possible. If you try to force them you will meet with disaster. But if brought along steadily, and given the treatment detailed previously in the book, they will yield crops much surer, cleaner, and a little earlier than the outdoor trees.

PART THREE
Melons and Strawberries

14—Melons

In the past we grew melons continuously in order to have supplies throughout the year. Their regular cultivation fell into disfavour when the contingencies of war made it impossible to supply the necessary artificial heat. Yet there are old greenhouses, and a few new ones, where they can be grown more successfully than tree fruit.

One point that may appeal to the modern trend is their quickness in fruiting. Seed is sown, the fruit gathered and the old vines destroyed all within from 16 to 20 weeks.

They are of the cucumber genus and need much the same conditions. But just as there are various types of cucumbers, so there are the distinct sorts of melons, and just a few varieties that belong to both, yet neither.

The main ones grown in greenhouses are the sweet, or musk, varieties, while the cantaloupes, or rock melons, are mostly grown in frames. The chief qualities are that sweet melons are more refined and subtle, compared with the stronger, coarser flavour and flesh of the cantaloupes.

Sweet Varieties

The choice of varieties is continually diminishing, yet there are still many with differing flesh colours, textures and flavours, as well as outward appearances. Most catalogues offer packets of mixed seed that are somewhat of a gamble, when you only need a few plants, and if they all grow you do not know which of the seedlings are best to plant in the beds for the crop.

The most reliable variety for a beginner is 'Hero of Lockinge'. It grows to a good size, has white flesh and a nicely netted skin. It is obtainable from most seedsmen. Varieties that have green flesh include 'Best of All', 'Emerald Green' and 'Ringleader'. Three with scarlet flesh are 'Blenheim Orange', 'Superlative' and 'King George'.

I

129

In the cantaloupe class is 'Charantais' that is rather small and has deep orange flesh. 'Dutch Net', or 'Spot', is another that is quite easy to grow and develops an ornamental skin that most other cantaloupes do not. 'Ogen' is a small variety considered to have the best flavour.

There are also some new F_1 hybrids likely to surpass the old varieties. One is 'Sweetheart' with a dull green skin, and scarlet flesh that is really sweet. Some will grow outdoors in a favourable year.

Water Melons

The term 'water melon' is often applied to sweet and cantaloupe melons quite wrongly. In America, some lists put them all under that category. But true water melons, such as grow in the fields in warmer climes, belong to an entirely different genus. Whereas all the sweet and cantaloupe melons are derived from *Cucumis melo*, the water melon is *Citrullus vulgaris*. A near relative of it is the Bitter Apple, or Bitter Cucumber, used as a laxative in medicine.

Hotbeds

Most large gardens of old included in the greenhouse range a forcing-pit, especially for growing cucumbers and melons. There was a footpath through the middle, or at the back, with a retaining brick wall up to 3 ft. high to make one side of a trough, the other side being the greenhouse wall. Sometimes warm pipes ran along the bottom of the trough, and sometimes the pipes were fixed to the greenhouse wall. The floor of the trough was about $2\frac{1}{2}$ ft. below the level of the eaves. When this was filled with hotbed material and soil, mounded up for each plant, the top of each mound came up close to the wire trellis fitted under the roof, as for vines and peaches. The trough was generally from $2-2\frac{1}{2}$ ft. wide from path to greenhouse wall.

Where there is a staging this is most times at the right height to form the floor of the trough. All that need be done is to put three layers of bricks along the front and back to make low walls for the trough. If the staging is slatted, some fine mesh wire, or similar material should be placed over it to stop soil falling through, and yet allow drainage. For solid staging, it is good to put a layer of rough pebbles or crocks over the bottom, and have the bricks spaced out so that any water can escape through the apertures.

Trellis

The melon plants must be trained to the wires, just as are tree fruits. These wires need to stretch end to end of the house, and there should be one vertical piece of bamboo or stick behind each plant up which the leading shoot can be trained and secured during its brief existence. (See Plate 5.)

Manure and Leaves

Most melons are grown on bottom heat. This means that the soil is heated by warmth coming from below. The old tried and trusted method is to obtain fresh horse manure, add some dead leaves that have not decayed, beech or oak being preferable, and mix and turn them all two or three times so that a heat is worked up. The leaves steady the heating of the manure and make it last longer. When ready, which is when the heat is just beginning to wane, it is placed inside the trough, filled almost to the top and beaten down firmly with the back of a fork.

Over that is placed the soil. This should not be too rich, for melons will not fruit well on too lush vines. Gardeners have their own recipes. A good one is to take a barrowload of soil from the kitchen garden, if it has been cultivated for a long time, or to obtain fresh, heavyish loam. Add two or three shovelfuls of old mortar rubble, or a little lime, a 5-in. potful of bonemeal, and a shovelful of small charcoal. Provided that the soil is deep enough for the roots not to touch the manure in the first place, there should be little trouble. In order to make sure that there are distinctive mounds, the hotbed material is humped so that there is a high point at every 2½ ft. of space. That is the best distance for planting. On top is put a layer of soil to cover the whole hot-bed surface, to an even depth of about 4 in., except the humps, where it is put 6 in. deep, so making, as it were, a series of large, flat-topped 'molehills' 2½ ft. apart.

Raising Seedlings

In the meantime, the seed can be sown, one in each 3-in. pot, usually having twice the number apparently needed. While melon seed does not often fail to germinate, it is rather erratic, therefore, if you sow twice as many as you need, there will be a choice of evenly grown plants at the time they must be put in the mounds. Some gardeners sow two seeds in each pot and remove the weaker one. I do not regard this as practical. The compost for the pots can be the sort generally used for most other seed.

More important is warmth and moisture. My method has been to put some moss in a shallow box, place the pots on this, cover the top with glass and paper and place on the warm water pipes, thus ensuring a temperature of about 65° F. (18° C.) by day and night. Enclosing the pots in this way ensures a retention of moisture; peat could be used instead of moss. Once germination is evident, as much light as possible is given, and warmth is continued, but they are moved away from the pipes. If no such facilities exist, there is no reason whatever why this method should not be copied in the home. Placed on a radiator and kept moistly warm, seed will soon respond. But plants must be moved to full light directly the first leaves form.

Once plants are well-rooted they should be planted without delay. Each is tipped out of its pot carefully and planted on its mound, so that the soil-surface when in the pot is well above the mound level. If planted deeply, this is inviting trouble.

Canker

Melons are prone to a canker disease that attacks the necks of the plants just above the roots. Where it has happened I have seen growers pile up lime around the stem, but it has not looked very nice. The best thing to do is try to avert it by planting shallowly and also by watering with Cheshunt Compound at the time of planting. Seeing that the life of the melon is so short, it is hardly worth trying to save them once this disease becomes bad. I think that it is often started by using the syringe too harshly on the lower parts of the plants while young, so allowing the bacteria to enter the bruised stems. There are theories that if you remove the soil from the roots lower down, so exposing them, they will become hard and resistent. While the roots will often come through the surface, through not having been planted very deeply in the first place, and the plants being on mounds, I much prefer not to tamper with them any more than is necessary.

Training

Having started the plants growing upon their mounds, by giving natural or artificial heat, and plenty of moisture, they will soon grow strongly, and the single stem should be guided up to the first horizontal wire by placing a bamboo cane behind it. Also, another cane can be fixed to the wires under the roof, to which the main stem can be lightly tied as it grows. Some people nip out the main tip and then have two stems side by side, but somewhat forked. However, I think it best to allow one stem to grow up to a height of about 3 ft. before nipping out the top. Side-shoots will form naturally, and as far as possible, it is good to train two of them to each wire, one to the left and one to the right of the main stem. If there are any surplus, they can be nipped off. When each side-shoot has grown $1\frac{1}{2}$ ft. its tip can likewise be nipped out.

Pollination

After a while, flowers will appear. Some will be male and some female, the latter having a tiny melon in globular form at the base. Those that have no such base are males. These are picked off, the yellow petals are removed and the pollen-bearing part is then pushed into the face of the female. The usual method is to leave each male flower on the female flower to wither at leisure.

Pollination should only be done while there are several female flowers in a similar state of development. Unless this is heeded the grower may be left with only one fruit, or two perhaps, that are equal in size. But if it is done at the right time it is possible to have at least four fruits on each plant. If there are more, the surplus can be thinned out later, as no plant can really yield more than four sizeable melons. Only one fruit should be allowed on any one shoot. Neither are any left to grow on the main stem.

The best time to pollinate is early morning, when the sun is shining, and when the atmosphere is comparatively dry. The house can be kept rather dry for two days at this period but should never be allowed to become really dried out.

The fruit having set, all other side-shoots should be pinched back as they form, but the growths upon which the fruits are borne must always be retained to their full length of $2\frac{1}{2}$ ft. so that the food is drawn to the fruits that will then take their share.

Spraying and Watering

A large measure of success depends upon watering and spraying. Whereas vines and peaches can be battered with water as it were, it should be more gently applied to melons and cucumbers. The modern mist propagation units could well be applied to the growing of these fruits.

As stated, spraying the stems at the base is dangerous in that it allows canker bacteria to enter slight wounds. I have seen gardeners put a very large-sized collar around the neck so that it protected them from spraying and yet allowed enough ventilation between stem and collar itself. Spraying should be carried out upon the main growths twice daily until flowering time. It is generally done when the house is warming up, and just before it is shut down at tea-time.

When the plants come into flower less water is given to the roots and the atmosphere is allowed to become a little drier. From the time the flowers have set until they begin to swell, moderate watering is given. The atmosphere is humid but not heavy. And when water is applied it should never be colder than tepid. Once they begin to swell, the air must then be charged with moisture until ripening is near, by spraying frequently. If at any time swelling melons do become dry and are then watered, there is a danger of fruits splitting.

Except when first planted, when a little shade can be given, they like all the sunshine available. Some growers give artificial shading, but if the ventilators are controlled correctly it is best not provided. At no time should the temperature be allowed to fall below 60° F. (16° C.) by night. If a thermostat heater is installed, it should be set at that control. By day, give a little ventilation when the thermometer registers 70° F. (21° C.) and then a little more when it is about 90° F. (33° C.) but partly shut down again directly it falls. It is all a matter of balanced sunshine and natural and artificial heat, together with a buoyant humid atmosphere.

When the fruits are getting to a nice size they will, if of the sweet varieties particularly, develop patterns on the skin which may perturb the uninitiated but are in fact the beginning of the process known as 'netting'. This is an ornamental crusting of the skin that seems to make them more relishable than they really are.

Supports

Netting should not be confused with the nets that are needed to support the fruits. These are supplied by specialist sundriesmen, such as Bentley's, and are like tiny hammocks, each 12 × 12 in., with corner strings to tie them up to the wire trellis so that each supports the fruit under which it is strung (see Plate 5).

Only when they are fully fruited, i.e. have three or four melons on each plant, is it advisable to give fertilisers. Just a little of one of the proprietary liquid plant foods added to the water once or twice just when they are swelling will help. But there is always the risk of over-feeding, and excessive watering that will cause splitting.

It will not be very long before the fruits start to mellow, and then watering should be diminished and spraying should be withheld. The foliage will turn yellow and the stalks begin to shrink, and there will be a musky aroma in the air. Keep the fruits on the vines in their tiny hammocks until they are quite ripe. The aroma will be stronger, and they can be tested by pressing the flat of the thumb gently into the end of the fruit opposite to the stalk. Keep them dry. When ripe this end will feel soft and rubbery. Another sign is the stalk starting to part from the fruit. Actually, I have seen it detach completely, and at one national show there was an exhibitor who stuck it on again, to gain the main award.

Alternative Methods

As revealed in these notes, melons must have warm nights and warmer days, and unless they can be assured it is hardly worth growing them. When lots of water pipes were universal, they were started in January, May, and August. Without artificial warmth it is unsafe to sow before the end of May. This ensures having the warmest four months, June to September, inclusive, in which to get a good crop. However, if a hotbed, as described, can be made for them, it is possible to start them in early May, and get a good crop early enough to be fully ripened and flavoured.

An alternative is to make up beds with decomposing straw. Bales should be obtained in the autumn, and loosened up. Sulphate of ammonia should be mixed into them so that by spring, or early summer, the decomposition has reached the stage in which the straw breaks up easily when handled. It is then used just as though it were hotbed material.

There are undersoil electric wires available that warm the soil, thus providing the 'bottom heat' so often mentioned in books and articles. The point about this is that the soil temperature should always be equal to, or higher than that of the atmosphere. This is the case with nearly all members of the cucumber and vegetable marrow family. Incidentally, it is much the same for mushrooms. They are crops that come naturally when the light is declining but the soil is warm and moist. Yet there must be sunshine for the melons, and plenty of fresh air, combined with humidity.

Cantaloupes

As far as I know, there is no reason why cantaloupe melons should not be grown in greenhouses, in the same way as the sweet musky varieties. But it is most usual to grow them in frames. The heap of warm materials is mounded in the middle of the frame. The lights are controlled so as to ensure night warmth, and day ventilation given after the temperature has reached about 75° F. (24° C.). They are watered when necessary, and syringed when the weather is very warm and drying. The main growths are allowed to grow towards each corner of the frame, and the tips nipped out when they have reached the sides. Side-shoots are controlled so that the mounded bed is nicely covered with foliage, but not so much that the flowers and fruits are shaded. Pollination is much the same as for the greenhouse varieties. Instead of a supporting net, it is usual to put a tile, or an inverted flower pot under each fruit when it has grown to a good size.

Diseases

The most likely trouble with melons, apart from canker, or collar rot already dealt with, is powdery mildew, which frequently appears when there is too much moisture in the air and not enough ventilation. There is also grey mould, or botrytis, that affects many greenhouse plants generally and is related to the mould upon strawberries outdoors in wet years. A proprietary fungicide containing dinocap, or sulphur, will bring mildew under control; captan or thiram will help with grey mould.

There are two serious diseases chiefly likely to appear in too cold conditions. They cause the roots to decay and the foliage to go yellow. They are of a fungal nature, as also is another bother known as leaf blotch. In the latter trouble the leaves have small spots that quickly spread, destroying all the foliage. There is nothing more to do than persist with Cheshunt Compound for root troubles and with sulphur when the leaves are affected.

The chief pest is red spider mite. But it will not appear if the growing conditions are kept moist enough. When it occurs in commercial cucumber houses there are a number of antidotes used, including azobenzene, petroleum oils and malathion. They are generally applied in the form of smokes or aerosals. But the melon, being such a short-lived one-crop fruit, is hardly worth saving from attacks of pests if water will not abate them. Red spider mite will often spread alarmingly during the ripening stage when no water is being applied. Little can be done except to clean out the house completely afterwards, burning all the old haulm.

15—Strawberries

Strawberries are not difficult to grow in any greenhouse, and as they do not take up much room, can be additional to other plants or fruit. Nevertheless, it is important to obtain the right plants and give them the proper treatment. As far as I know, it is impossible to take more than one good yield from any of them.

There are two types of plants from which greenhouse crops can be obtained. At one time it was thought best to grow them for about a year and a half before forcing, keeping them in pots the whole time. The first year's flowers were removed, so that they built up into substantial specimens for the proper season. But the more popular way is to take very early rooted runners in late July and grow these on so that they bear fruit indoors during April or May.

There is no doubt that the plants propagated in one's own garden are best, but only if they are healthy and really fully developed. If they are not healthy and fully grown it is better to buy some from a most reliable nurseryman who has really rooted them in pots, instead of just taken field runners and potted them up, which I have known to be done.

It is assumed that the reader knows how to grow outdoor strawberries. If not, there are books available regarding their cultivation, and before anyone attempts to grow outdoor crops, whether for normal outdoor cropping, or for raising plants for forcing, it is essential to know how to treat them.

Varieties

There is no doubt whatever that the best strawberry ever raised is 'Royal Sovereign', and it forces well. But there are so few healthy stocks of it about that the beginner, particularly, is unlikely to obtain a suitable strain. Apart from this one, very few varieties last more than a small number of years, being continuously superseded by newcomers. Yet I feel that 'Cambridge

Vigour' will remain for a long time, it being resistant to red core and virus-tolerant. It is good for forcing. Another is 'Cambridge Rival'.

As everyone should know, strawberry plants increase by runners that emanate from the mother plants in late June or July, or later. The best runners come from one-year-old parents. The procedure is to remove the flowers from the maiden year-old plants so that they either develop into good plants, for fruiting a year later, or they produce excellent early runners. These runners are pegged down into small pots of lightish soil that are sunk into the strawberry bed around the mother plant. If any secondary runners grow from the first rootling, they are nipped off. Once the roots have filled the pots, the plants are severed from their parents, and placed in a semi-shady place, where they are put closely together and kept watered as necessary. They are then ready for planting in the garden, or for growing on for greenhouse fruiting.

If for the greenhouse they are re-potted in August, putting them in those of 6 in. diameter, and planting so that the crowns or tops of the clumps are slightly above the soil surface level. There should be about a ½ in. space between the top of the pot rim and the surface of the soil in the pot.

A most suitable compost is 3 parts turfy loam, of medium texture, 1 part decayed manure, or sedge peat, 1 part mortar rubble, with brickdust in it if possible (parts by bulk), and just a little bonemeal, and fine charcoal. Put drainage crocks in the pots, and over them a little coarse peat before filling with the compost. When tipping out of the small pots, slightly crack the crusted surface of the root ball, but do not entirely break it up. Keep the crown of each plant just clear of the soil surface. Stand the pots back in a semi-shady place on an ash bed, or hard natural floor. I have often put them on a gravel path. They are never allowed to become dry, and when the weather is warm in late summer are frequently syringed.

After about a fortnight, they are transferred to a sunny place, preferably a cold frame. They should be kept moderately watered. Some growers also give them light doses of soot water, or a weak liquid fertiliser. Keep them well ventilated until the cold weather comes. And only put the lights over them when frosts are severe, or there is too much rain. Put ventilation on by blocking up the glass lights on the windward side. The plants should always be kept as near the glass as possible without it touching the leaves. They are kept like that until January or February.

When the houses are being warmed up in February, as is the case with vines and peaches, a batch of the pots are transferred to them, being put, for preference, on shelves close up under the roof. The later they are placed in heat the easier they are to crop. But if started in January they will produce strawberries in April.

The temperature to start them should not be above 50° F. (10° C.) by night and a little warmer by day. As they grow, so can the heat be gradually increased. They love a moistish air, such as is being given to the peaches or vines, and if they are being grown in another sort of house, it is something to be remembered.

When the flowers open they have to be pollinated. It is best done by daubing every one with a camel-hair brush, or rabbit's tail. At this time, the air should be drier and they are best not watered too heavily. But when not in flower, they can be syringed frequently, if it is possible to reach them.

Once fruit has set, and it has done so very liberally, they should be thinned out so that there are no more than eight berries on a vigorous plant, or six on a medium one.

When the fruit is beginning to swell, a weak dose of liquid fertiliser once a week will help considerably. To keep the fruit clear of the pot and the compost, the stalks are held up by small forked twigs, similar to the wooden part of a catapult. When the first fruit changes colour, and it can be managed, ventilation should be more freely given, and all spraying stayed. If they are in a vinery or peach house and can be moved elsewhere, it is advisable to do so. If not, they should be put as near the ventilator as possible.

A likely trouble is greenfly. It is best to use a non-persistent aerosol, such as malathion which is simply applied from a push-button canister, and it should be prevented as far as possible from contacting the fruit. It also deals with the other possible pest, the usual red spider mite.

Strawberries have many diseases. When grown in the fields particularly, and in the garden to a lesser degree, to know about these and how to counter them is essential. But for greenhouse work it is better to ignore them. If the plants are healthy to begin with these troubles are unlikely to occur. If they do it is hardly worth the effort to struggle against them. Far more practical is it to throw out any sick crops, clean the surroundings, and try again.

A proverbial ambition is to have ripe strawberries for Christmas. It can be done if they are given a warm greenhouse throughout November and December. But the process takes longer. Instead of fruiting new runners in the pots the plants have to be kept for over a whole year, i.e. a season, longer.

It is best to use early varieties. The runners are rooted in pots on the outdoor beds during July and August, and are given the precise treatment already described for the April fruiting kinds up to the point of getting those ready for the greenhouse, but at that stage they are, instead of being put in the greenhouse, plunged in an ash or peat bed, up to the pot rims, and kept growing outdoors in an open position throughout the spring, summer and autumn to come.

All flower stalks and runners are scrupulously picked off. They are watered as necessary and occasionally sprayed with insecticide as well as given occasional weak doses of weak fertiliser in solution.

In early October, which is 15 months after being rooted from runners, they are partly shaded by day, and left fully exposed at night. Frosts are most helpful at this time. The object is to cheat the plants into thinking that it is winter. They are kept like that until the beginning or middle of November. When then moved into the greenhouse, they are placed on sunny shelves and subjected to a temperature of about 50° F. (10° C.). This should not be exceeded, except when the sun raises it naturally.

When the flower stems appear they are given the treatment already described, i.e. pollination and so on. And the plants are given a phosphatic fertiliser every few days according to their vitality. The stronger they are the more food will they take. I have used phosphate of potash, not giving more than a teaspoonful in a gallon of tepid water, for nine or ten plants, taking care to not wet the plants, and always doing it when the soil is already thoroughly moist.

No doubt, by modern methods of giving fluorescent lighting, this process can be put upon a more scientific basis. It must be remembered that light has a major effect upon these plants. It is far more important than heat. Excessive warmth is dangerous.

In recent years, the remontant, or perpetual-fruiting strawberries have come to the fore, and it may be possible to persuade these to defer their fruiting until Christmas, by carefully removing all the flowers in the early part of the season and then placing them in gentle warmth when the fruit is required. It is an idea that could be pursued.

Supplementary Notes

Greenhouses

The manufacture of greenhouses is a large industry, involving those that are of gigantic sizes for commercial production, down to tiny ones intended to cater for the many people who have a hazy ambition to own one. Obviously, some of the latter are excellent and the makers have given much thought to the wares they sell, while others are cheap and shoddy and only lead to despondency.

The old days when expense was of little account have gone, yet in my opinion, the traditional wooden framed structure of that era with the solid lower half of walling has yet to be improved upon—if for fruit trees. This is applicable for either a lean-to or span.

But the elaborate water-pipe heating with the stoke-hole boiler and the consequent necessity of unremitting attention has become redundant. In large nurseries where economics are decisive, thermostat oil heating has become general, and with other automatic aids the amount and the degree of labour involved has become much minimised.

Up to just recently, most forms of automation have been too costly or elaborate for small garden greenhouses, but some are now being developed for gardeners, both professional and amateur, that should be borne in mind when choosing a new greenhouse of whatever size, or shape.

Nevertheless, while new aids will alleviate the old problems of providing warmth, ventilation, water, drainage, and feeding the occupants, they will never completely eradicate them.

There are firms fully conversant with the needs of special crops, who specialise in making large or small houses to customers' requirements. They may be a little more costly than the mass-produced patterns, but will prove 'cheapest in the end'. The manufacturers of individually designed houses have much experience in the siting of them and have gained extensive knowledge concerning the needs of the plants and trees to be grown.

However, we must here consider some of the many types of mass-produced greenhouses, and see how they can be adapted to suit grapes, peaches or figs. Even if you do not wish to grow fruit, the structural alterations that are advised will be just as beneficial for other plants.

Undoubtedly, the chief drawback of many small greenhouses is insufficient ventilation. I have sketched nine examples that are more or less representative of present availability (see Fig. 18). If you have read the second chapter of the book they can be compared with the ideal vinery (Fig. 1).

There are some of excellent design, and ideal for plants. Such as these are best for flowers, and need no modifications. If owners cannot manage them they cannot manage anything, even for fruit. But they often have metal or aluminium frames, and our problem here is to fix the wire trellis that is essential for all vines, trees, and melons, when the roots are in beds or borders rather than receptacles.

But even when they are ideal for plants, they need heat, and that is often denied them during the winter months when it is needed most whereas, if fruit is grown by the methods described in this book, it is advisedly unnecessary. The owner who finds it impossible to supply heat during the winter months for other crops can either grow the fruit in pots, or investigate the possibilities of fitting the trellis to the framework. Although problematic, nothing of this sort is impossible if one has the tenacity.

The chief problems of greenhouse management are interrelated and concern the atmosphere. This should be of a humidity density pleasing to the plants, and of a temperature that they like in their natural state. It is brought about by the application of water, and the control of air by circulation, ventilation, artificial warmth, sun warmth and shading, if necessary. For fruit the last can be entirely eliminated.

The control of air warmth and circulation has chiefly been by means of ventilators letting it flow in below and escaping at the top. That is where many modern greenhouses are lacking. This can often be overcome by electric turbo-heaters, so frequently mentioned in previous chapters, and which have made a vast difference to airing problems. Many damping-off diseases and even fungal bothers are eliminated if the fan is working, whether or not heat is on as well. They are ideal for fruit houses and overcome many of the shortcomings of some of the greenhouses in the examples.

Ventilators

But the thermostat heater, plus automatic fan, is not always a complete solution. Although it reduces scorch proneness in the height of summer when the sun shines on foliage and fruit in a condensed atmosphere, the top ventilators should be opened directly the inside temperature rises, and at one time this was a constant worry. Once the gardener failed to awaken on a bright sunny morning, considerable damage was done.

It is now possible to fit automatic ventilator openers that can be set to work at any thermostat temperature. They are completely independent of electricity or any power source. The reader is advised strongly to study the various models available.

With the temporary thermostatic heater, the fan and the automatic ventilator opener, many of the houses need no more modifications. Those marked (c), (d), (e), (g) and (j) will then be most suitable for fruit if only the wire trellis can be fitted.

But (a), (b) and (h) need wall ventilators that can be opened by hinged lids or sliding panels so that there is a through circulation when fruit is ripening. Note that the sloping sides of (h) are fixed, but if they could be made to open and close without much trouble it would be good, and obviate having wall ventilators.

Pattern (f) needs a comment all to itself. While it is quite good for vines or trees, there must be additional ventilation possibilities somewhere. The ideal is to fit louvres at the sides after the manner of pattern (d). If that is impossible, it may be feasible to lift the whole frame on to a brick base and have air ventilators along the bottom, with sliding or hinged covers. In that case, the whole inside bed could also be raised by building an inside retaining wall as shown in the ideal vinery. This type of house gives plenty of light and maximum room commensurate with size, and when the framework is of wood, the iron bars for the wires can be drilled and screwed to the main frame at the ends to strengthen the whole structure. (See Chapter 2, Fig. 3.)

FIG. 18. Typical greenhouses

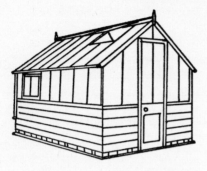

(a) A typical small half-glazed greenhouse with top and side ventilators

(b) A standard greenhouse
with three-quarter glazing
and top ventilators

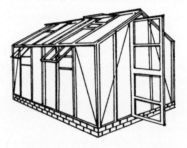

(c) The metal framework and full
glazing of this house ensure
maximum light

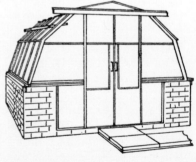

(d) Greenhouse with sliding door

(e) Greenhouse with brick/glass sides
and sliding door

(f) House of Dutch lights with sliding door

(g) Greenhouse with wood/glazed sides

(h) House with brick/glazed sides, the glass being sloping

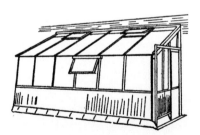

(j) Lean-to against brick wall

Wire Trellis

Another problem for many small houses is the fitting of the horizontal wires about 8 in. apart, that extend from one end to the other, several inches from the glass roof and sides, which I have frequently referred to as the trellis. Where the aluminium frames of the structure are significantly thin it may be unwise and impracticable to attach them to the main body. Rather, it may be better to use iron bars with these base ends set in concrete that will remain steady and unyielding. Then if there are any means of attaching the top ends to the roof this can be done merely to steady the trellis rather than to support it.

This problem should first be taken up with the manufacturers. Sometimes they will brush off the inquiry, but often they will be helpful, and occasionally can supply the necessary fittings. Otherwise, the local blacksmith, who is generally capable and obliging, will accept this sort of job as a challenge to his ingenuity.

For very small houses, such as depicted in patterns (a) and (b) only two or three horizontal wires are necessary on each side of the structure, if it is to be used for vines, although six or more are needed for peaches and figs. Iron stays or bars bolted to the wooden ends, with eye-holes at the right places for wires, are easy to fix, and will strengthen rather than weaken the structure.

Training Policy

For peaches, nectarines and figs, only the fan-trained form of tree is practicable. For vines, most often, in small houses, the best system is the horizontal rod one, as practised in the largest vineries, including that at Hampton Court. The main stem can be grown from an outside bed through the south end of the house, and then inside it can branch off into as many rods as there is room for. The topmost pair are parallel, just under the inside apex, and others are spaced 2 ft. asunder below to within $2\frac{1}{2}$–3 ft. from the floor. The patterns of houses where this is most applicable are (a), (b) and (g).

For the other patterns, it is probably better to have upright triple-rods, i.e. from the stump they divide into three branches (or rods) like a toasting-fork. This is particularly so if there is enough room for an inside border, or one that is 'inside-cum-outside'.

Borders

For peaches that must be inside, it is possible to increase the border area by allowing the roots to grow both inside and under the wall to the outside by making borders in the proper way, but instead of having the elaborate arches of the ideal vinery type, there can be solid brick underground columns, or stilts inside the border to support the house, and concrete rails placed across the stilts to fit and support the base of the houses. This can be done to both wooden and metal framed structures.

For vines this method can also be adopted, but when structures are so small, the best answer is to keep the whole of the borders outside. But in the case of pattern (f) the border can be raised over the whole of the inside, and covered with duckboard to make a path.

It is hoped that these ideas, combined with cultivations, will help the grower to overcome the difficulties, whatever they are. They need some scheming, but they can be solved by thought and application.

As a last resort, of course, it is possible to grow all the fruit in large pots, and carry them in and outdoors when they need it, as explained earlier. But they do need more frequent attention than trees completely planted in borders. However, figs are very good subjects with which to do this and benefit from that sort of treatment.

Watering

Watering the roots, and supplying moisture to the atmosphere, can be made much easier by adopting one or other of the various systems now coming into favour. Mist propagation has been around a long time, but I do not think it the answer to fruit cultivation unless the roots are also watered whenever necessary. But there are trickle irrigation systems that need the fullest consideration. All the manufacturers in the appendices should be consulted, and each system studied.

One of the problems is that there are times when it is better to have dry conditions, and others when humidity is desirable. These are explained for the various fruits earlier and should be heeded. But I am not so sure that the latest humidity meters are of much use to indoor fruit growers. They turn the fun of growing into a science and if mistakes occur the outcome is heart-breaking.

Old gardeners get the 'feel' of the atmosphere when they walk into the greenhouse and know just when it is right or wrong. That feeling is more reliable than an instrument that you must inspect anyway, to find out. I would rather rely upon my reactions to the prevailing state of warmth and humidity than that of any meter that does not change according to circumstances.

There are several systems of applying water to the soil. Some involve capillary dampness, and hardly help us. The ones we need should release varying degrees of water through drip taps, or inject moisture into the atmosphere somewhat heavier in density than mist so that they soak the border when they need it most, but can be adjusted so that they do it according to prevailing needs. They should release enough moisture to keep the atmosphere buoyantly humid in the growing periods, and they should be adjustable, so that when the grower walks into the house he can instantly alter the switch, just as in the same way he knows when his drawing-room is too stuffy, or too cold, or whatever the case may be. Generally, unless you are an exceptional person, plants like the conditions that suit you. But you must also know when they need more or less than usual in due season.

One of the problems of mechanical watering is the temperature of the water being colder than that of the greenhouse. It mostly comes from the mains. If it is possible, the rainwater off the roof should be collected inside the small house and applied with a watering-can to the borders. Or if there is a moisture releasing system, it should be on the lavatory cistern principle, but instead of there being a rapid flush it is slowly released from nozzles into the atmosphere.

If it is home-saved soft water, it is necessary to fill the cistern from time to time, but if from the mains, fed straight to the cistern, it does at least become partly acclimatised to the greenhouse before being released. For at each release, only a small part of the contents of the cistern is expended.

Alas, the saving of water, as was included in the design for the ideal vinery is often completely ignored in the cheap greenhouses. The rain off the roof, or the sloping sides simply falls to the ground, not doing the foundations, nor the beds, any good whatever. This is another point to look for when buying a greenhouse.

But where the cheap product is being converted it is very worth while fitting rain gutters if possible, and collecting the water either indoors, or outside. There are light plastic gutters available from most builders' merchants which are easy to fit, and not very expensive.

Thermometers

These were the first automatic aids the greenhouse owner used. When one enters, one usually glances at the temperature reading. If a guess is made as to what it would be before checking, it would probably be a few degrees above or below, due to the outdoor influences. On a cold windy day the recording could be lower than you thought it was. On a warm day, it may be higher. Yet, one's own feelings are a closer guide to what the plants need than is a close adherence to fixed temperatures, such as are given by thermostat controls. While thermostats in their increasing variations are undoubtedly a godsend to the veriest beginner and the person who has to leave the greenhouse to its own devices most of the time, that small degree of discretion brings the very best results.

If the greenhouse is ventilated by knowing precisely what is good for the plants, just as one habitually opens the windows of the home, without due regard to exact temperatures, but taking into consideration the weather as it is momentarily, and how it is likely to develop in an hour or two's time, one is becoming a grower of understanding.

Our outdoor vegetation stands up to the vagaries of the weather much better than anyone would think. It is only extreme drought, or storms, or frost that kills, or severely injure. These extremes can also occur in a small greenhouse in fact, the temperatures can soar to much greater heights and fall almost as low as those outdoors if there are no controls. Greenhouse cultivation is actually a modification of extremities by adjustments, either by thermostats, or by human judgment. The latter can be better than mechanical controls but, until one gets the feeling of it all, it can be far, far worse.

Aerosols

Mention was made in the text of aerosol controls of pests. This involves the fitting of an appliance thermostatically heated by electricity that emits vapour into the atmosphere, charged with insecticides, or fungicides, according to the pests to be destroyed. I have worked in houses where they have been in constant use for over 20 years, and felt no ill effects. Before they were instituted, we used insecticides such as fumigant tobacco shreds, and liquid azobenzene sprays, in largish quantities that really never cleared persistent pests like white-fly. The saving in chemicals since the aerosols were used has been miraculous. Those from the aerosols are so minute, that one hardly detects their presence, their continuity being the complete eradication of trouble such as red spider mite and mildew.

The danger of using them lies only in the possibility that the grower will not then give his subjects the proper attention. For example, the trees and vines need moisture in the atmosphere and benefit with spraying. It is known that red spider mite is eliminated by water. If an aerosol also does it, spraying should not be neglected.

Earlier, mention has been made of malathion which is about the mildest of the many organophosphorous compounds that disperse after a few days. This, as far as I know, cannot be used in the electric dispensers. But it is obtainable in the form of smoke fumigants. If used carefully there is no danger whatever to anything other than the pests to be killed. One would not, naturally, stay in such an atmosphere to see what it felt like. After a few hours the ventilators can be opened and the chemical completely dispersed.

Automatic Feeding

There are also drip systems of watering that can be made good use of, in which it is possible to add dilute quantities of fertiliser. But it should be remembered that such things do not make weak plants strong unless they are merely starving. Unhealthy plants generally have something wrong with them that must be put right before they can take much food.

There are also feeds that are sprayed on to the leaves and stems. These are excellent if the roots are right. They should not be regarded as alternatives for bad roots. The best time to use them is after an attack of pests, such as red spider mite, or should the leaves have been scorched by accident. I regard foliar feeds as plant tonics rather than desirable permanent fare.

In recent times, the use of carbon dioxide has become popular in large nursery glasshouses. It is released into the atmosphere by thermostatic control, and is associated with other precepts of automation. It has to be done precisely, or plants and humans can suffer.

There is an idea that this can also help the small greenhouse owner. I understand that rubber bags can be filled by squirting soda syphon bulbs into them which are then fitted with a very fine release nozzle. Whether this works out satisfactorily in a small fruit house I do not know.

Other such aids are coming along thick and fast. Some will be very good, and others not. I think they are well worth investigating, and if feasible, trying, if not adopting. Anything that will lessen the chores and improve the quality is welcome. For all that, if the fundamental needs of plants of any description are not heeded, no gadgets will ever replace them.

Appendix

Addresses of companies that can be useful to cultivators of fruit in greenhouses

Please note that neither by inclusion, nor omission, must the name of any firm be regarded as a recommendation, or otherwise. It is probable that local suppliers can offer similar products, and give better service. The list is primarily for those who do not know where to go. They must themselves compare quality and prices.

Nurseries

Vines   There are many firms that supply 'Black Hamburgh', but comparatively few who offer other varieties. Some that do are:

> S. E. Lytle Ltd.,
> Park Road,
> Formby,
> Lancs

> C. & A. and L. J. Poole,
> Oakleigh,
> Green Lane,
> Chessington,
> Surrey

> Thomas Rivers and Son Ltd.,
> The Nurseries,
> Sawbridgeworth,
> Herts

> Pine Nurseries,
> Rotherfield,
> Crowborough,
> Sussex

Peach, Nectarine and *Fig Trees*	Laxton Bros. Ltd., Brampton Nurseries, Huntingdon
	Merryweather and Sons Ltd., Southwell, Notts
	Thomas Rivers and Sons Ltd., Sawbridgeworth, Herts
	John Scott and Co. Ltd., Merriott, Somerset

(There are many other good nurseries.)

Strawberries These are freely available, but it may be difficult to obtain early-rooted runners in pots ready to be replanted into larger pots.
Some likely sources are:

> Ken Muir,
> Honeypot Fruit Farm,
> Clacton-on-Sea,
> Essex

> B. G. Plummer and Son,
> Southlands,
> Oakhanger, Bordon,
> Hants

Melons Seed obtainable from Sutton and Sons Ltd., Reading, Berks., and many other firms.

Greenhouses

When buying greenhouses for special purposes it is essential to study all the features, to see whether they are entirely suitable. The following brief list in no way indicates the type or patterns of the greenhouses made by the manufacturers. These should be fully investigated, not only regarding special features, but quality and prices. Some firms also offer ancillary equipment.

Alitex Ltd.,
Station Road,
Alton,
Hants

Alton Greenhouses Ltd.,
Alton Works,
Bewdley,
Worcs

Hartley Clear Span Ltd.,
Wellington Road,
Greenfield,
Nr. Oldham,
Lancs

Midcon Ltd.,
Masons Road,
Stratford-on-Avon,
Warks

H. E. Phillips Ltd.,
King William Street,
Coventry,
Warks

F. Pratten & Co. Ltd.,
Charlton Road,
Midsomer Norton,
Bath,
Somerset

G. F. Strawson & Son,
St. Andrew's Works,
Charlesfield Road,
Horley,
Surrey

Worth Buildings Ltd.,
Donnington,
Wellington,
Salop

Manufacturers of Various Ancillary Equipment

Messrs. Humex Ltd.,
5 High Road,
Byfleet,
Weybridge,
Surrey

Shepherd's Aerosols Ltd.,
Shernfold Park,
Frant,
Tunbridge Wells,
Kent

Simplex of Cambridge Ltd.,
Sawston,
Cambridge

Suppliers of Special Needs, such as Grape Scissors, Styptic, etc.

Messrs. Joseph Bentley Ltd.,
Barrow-on-Humber,
Lincolnshire

Note: Fertilisers and pesticides manufactured by large firms such as PBI, ICI, Fison's, Shell, Murphy's, etc., are stocked by most sundriesmen, or if there is any difficulty can be obtained from Joseph Bentley (above).

Index